MALE DOMINANCE
AND FEMALE AUTONOMY

Domestic Authority in Matrilineal Societies

ALICE SCHLEGEL

with a foreword by
RAOUL NAROLL

HRAF PRESS   1972

ABOUT THE AUTHOR

Alice Schlegel received her M.A. from the University of Chicago and her Ph.D. from Northwestern University. She is presently assistant professor of anthropology at the University of Pittsburgh. Her interest in matrilineal societies began with her fieldwork among the Hopi Indians. She has spent two summers on the Hopi reservation, with continued contacts, both on the reservation and in town, during the three years she lived in Flagstaff, Arizona. Her current interests are cross-cultural research, the anthropology of women, and Hopi kinship and cosmology.

LIBRARY OF CONGRESS CATALOG CARD NUMBER: 72-78401
© COPYRIGHT 1972
HUMAN RELATIONS AREA FILES, INC.
ALL RIGHTS RESERVED

TO MY MOTHER

Contents

Figures

Tables

Foreword

Raoul Naroll

This hologeistic study by Alice Schlegel offers some fresh insights and some hard evidence on two classic anthropological puzzles—the matrilineal puzzle and the incest taboo puzzle. I predict that this book will be much cited, much discussed in years to come.

In her study of the matrilineal puzzle, Schlegel highlights the topic of men's authority over grown women—men's authority over wives and men's authority over sisters. Her insights on the importance of authority over grown women go far to resolve the much discussed question of unilateral cross-cousin marriage. Schlegel classifies men's authority over adult women into a five-level scale:

Type I—strong husband authority; no brother authority

Type II—some brother authority but husband authority predominant

Type III—authority of husband and brother about equal

Type IV—some husband authority but brother authority predominant

Type V—strong brother authority; no husband authority

The application of this typology to her sample of 66 matrilineal societies yielded two important findings:

A. Type III societies, where authority of husband and brother were about equal, usually turned out to be societies where the total authority of men over women was least. In Type III societies, the women are in a position to play off brother against husband, and they do so. Schlegel's own considerable field work among the Type III Hopi enabled her to watch this process at work.

B. Unilateral cross-cousin marriages of both sorts turn out to reflect a single underlying principle. Both sorts of marriages tend to be marriages in which an older male brings a bridegroom over whom he has influence because of his family tie into a marriage with a woman over whom he has authority—into a domestic group over which he has authority. Matrilateral cross-cousin marriages tend to occur most frequently in Type I and II societies, where the authority of a woman's husband predominates over that of her brother. In such a situation, Schlegel points out, matrilateral cross-cousin marriage amounts to a marriage where Old Man Ego brings his sister's son into the domestic group over which he has authority, his wife's. Patrilateral cross-cousin marriages tend to occur most frequently in Type IV and V societies, where the authority of a woman's brother predominates over that of her husband. In this case, a patrilateral cross-cousin marriage amounts to a marriage where Old Man Ego brings his own son into the domestic group over which he has authority, his sister's.

Schlegel's study also contributes to the analysis of a second classic problem in the comparative ethnology of the family—the incest taboo. Schlegel's inquiry here led her to classify the relative strength of incest taboos of two leading types: father-daughter taboos and sister-brother taboos. She finds that in her 66 matrilineal societies, the strength of these taboos tends to vary as the familial authority pattern varies. Where the dominant familial pattern is Type I or Type II (husband dominant), the father-daughter taboo is stronger than the sister-brother taboo. But in Types IV and V societies (brother-dominant), it is the other way around: the sister-brother taboo is stronger than the father-daughter taboo. Thus these human arrangements contradict the principle of sexual dominance found in many species of monkeys and apes. Among these other primates, sexual dominance is used to reinforce and strengthen—to echo—status, authority, and dominance. But among human societies, the greater the authority of the man over his potential sexual partner, the more the incest taboos tighten to provide greater resistance to sexual access.

Methodologically, this study of Schlegel's is well designed. Her sample nearly consisted of one representative from each of Murdock's 73 culture clusters in which a matrilineal society occurred. She gave careful attention to the nature of each ethnic unit—its structure and its time focus. (But she did not look at community focus or at the double language boundary question—refinements which were not current when she planned her work.) She documents her codings elaborately—giving precise page citations for each of her coding decisions. She publishes her coding manual; and nearly all her codings were checked by a naive coder. She drew on Murdock for some of her variables, rather than coding them originally; but here she systematically checked his codings herself, and corrected a number of them, as she sets forth in detail. She ran formal data quality control tests, using these control factors: (1) quantity of data (2) quality of data, and (3) sex of major researcher. Coder reliability was tested and proved satisfactory—usually above 80 percent agreement. Schlegel also tested her key variables for regional association; she found some clustering of traits by continent, but not enough to support the rival hypothesis that her results were mere regional artifacts. This finding was reinforced by her linked pair tests for diffusion—Galton's problem; these results too were reassuring; she found no more frequent associations in all her linked pair tests than would be expected by chance from random numbers codings.

She dealt adequately with the group significance problem—the "combing," "dredging," or "mudsticking" problem, as it has been variously termed. Do her "statistically significant" results merely reflect selection by her of a few fortuitously unusual results from a much larger number of correlations? This problem is especially pressing when one is reporting the results of a large number of correlations run by tireless computers. In all, she ran 76 correlations involving her main theoretical variable—domestic authority pattern. Of these 76 correlations, 33 proved statistically significant at the 5 percent level. How likely would she have been to get 23 such results if she had been running a like set of tests with nonsense data—data from tables of random numbers? Where $N = 70$ and $p = 0.5$, the randomly expected frequency is, of course, 3.5. Under the mudsticking null hypothesis, we would not expect to get 23 such results in one run of 76 correlations out of ten *billion* such runs (Weintraub 1963: 556, $N = 76$, $R = 21$, $P = .05$).

Finally, Schlegel seeks assiduously among the deviant cases in her sample to explain conspicuous "misses"—i.e. to explain conspicuous exceptions to her theoretical models.

All in all, Schlegel's study makes a solid contribution to hologeistic literature.

REFERENCE CITED

Weintraub, Sol
  1963 *Tables of the cumulative binomial probability distribution for small values of p*, New York, Free Press.

Preface

Like many students of anthropology, I had clear ideas about the nature of matrilineal society. After a summer's fieldwork among a matrilineal people, the Hopi, I discovered that many of these ideas were wrong. I became convinced that there were some rather broad areas of matrilineal kinship that needed investigation, and the result was this study. It deals with domestic group organization, an area which has been somewhat overlooked in the theoretical literature on matrilineality, in favor of lineage and clan structure. I focus on one dimension of domestic organization, the power-authority relationship between the key adults in the domestic group.

This work would have been impossible without the help and stimulus of others, and I take this opportunity to express my thanks and gratitude. Ronald Cohen has so often performed the difficult task of being simultaneously supportive and critical, and it is from him that my interest in power as one aspect of human relationships stems. I have been strongly influenced by Francis Hsu's work on dyadic relationships within the kinship circle. To Raoul Naroll I owe training in cross-cultural method, and this study has profited much from his suggestions. He contributed directly to it by conducting the Linked Pair test (see Chapter 5), for which I am grateful. With Oswald Werner and Joann Fenton I have shared ideas on matrilineal society.

Others, also, have been of help to me, and I owe them my heartfelt thanks. Nancy Tanner took the time to discuss with me in some detail the traditional and contemporary conditions in Minangkabau. William Davenport kindly coded Santa Cruz for me. My graduate assistant, Larry Armstrong, worked on this study as co-coder with intelligence and concern. I wish to thank William Klecka for his kindness in instructing a novice in the mysteries of the computer. And finally, I am grateful to Audrey Thomas for her help in preparing the manuscript.

Much of the planning and research for this study was done while I was on a National Institute of Mental Health Predoctoral Fellowship. I thankfully acknowledge the support I have received.

Male Dominance
and Female Autonomy

Matrilineal Kinship and the Problem
of Domestic Authority[1]

Matrilineal kinship has exerted a fascination for Western-
ers steeped in a bilateral, patriarchal tradition. The difficulty in comprehending the rationale of such a descent
system is reflected in the older literature by the concept of
matriarchy, as if women who were not under the control of
their husbands were naturally in control of them—an interesting comment on the cultural belief in the latent power
of women, perhaps, but not very accurate. In the more recent literature, the ease with which Richards' (1950) phrase
"matrilineal puzzle" has taken hold suggests that the system
is still not well understood: What may be a puzzle to the
Western ethnographer is simply a fact of social organization
to the native, no more and no less puzzling than any other
fact of organization.

The earliest works concerning matrilineality were those
which confused matrilineality with matriarchy and considered both to be an early stage in man's evolutionary history. The most famous of these is Bachofen's *Das Mutter-
recht* (1861). (For a discussion of these early works, see
Murdock 1949: 184-87.)

---

[1] This chapter is a revision and expansion of a paper read at the
68th Annual Meetings of the American Anthropological Association,
New Orleans, 1969, and published in the *Steward Journal of Anthropology 1*: 121-28, 1970.

As more field studies were accomplished, the error
this notion became apparent. By 1924, Hobhouse said:

> What is really common among the simpler peoples, is not matri-
> archy, but mother-right, and along with mother-right, and
> where it most flourishes, it is perfectly possible for the position
> of women to be as low as the greatest misogynist could desire.
> ... The woman is not necessarily any better off because she is
> ruled by a brother in place of a husband [1924: 159-60].

One of the first attempts to study matrilineal societ
systematically is the neglected work of Ronhaar, *Woman
Primitive Motherright Societies* (1931). In this study, t
author looks at characteristics of matrilineal societies cro
culturally. Unfortunately, Ronhaar's sample is poorly cc
structed, with no recognition of the problem of diffusi
(see Chapter 3). It is also geographically restricted, f
with the exception of Iroquoian peoples, the societies in
sample are all from the Circum-Pacific region. There
other methodological and theoretical points on which t
work can be faulted, but it is a landmark in the history
matrilineal studies, and of systematic cross-cultural resear
as well. It deserves to be better known.

Matrilineal studies were considerably advanced by t
publication of Richards' paper on family structure amc
the Central Bantu (1950). This was a major step in refin
analysis of the varieties of social organization within t
framework of a matrilineal descent system. For Richar
the critical factor in determining social organization is re
dence. She states:

> These variations in the family structure depend largely on the
> nature of the marriage contract and the extent to which the
> husband is able to gain control over his wife, who belongs, by
> virtue of matrilineal descent, to the lineage and clan of her
> mother and of her brothers and sisters; and also on the extent to
> which he manages to achieve a position of authority over the
> children she bears. ... In this balance of privileges and duties
> between the patrikin and the matrikin the crucial point is ob-
> viously the husband's right to determine the residence of the
> bride [Richards 1950: 208].

In patrilineal societies, the organization of the domes
group reinforces the organization of the descent group. T

domestic group, or household, is the minimal segment of the descent group, and the only nonlineal kin of importance within it, the wife/mother, has little or no official voice in running its affairs. The descent group is maintained and perpetuated by the very men who are in authority within the domestic group. In matrilineal societies, on the other hand, there is a division of these roles. The descent group is perpetuated by women. However, it is men who are the heads of descent groups, and usually of domestic groups as well. This dispersal of roles, and the need to coordinate them into a working system, led Richards to coin the phrase "matrilineal puzzle."

She saw four solutions to this puzzle (Richards 1950: 246-48). Each involved a different residence pattern, bringing together into a day-to-day, cooperative unit different segments of lineal and affinal kin. Her typology is as follows:

1. The matriarchal solution, in which house and lands pass through the women and are managed by the brother. Two examples of this are the Nayar, in which husbands visit wives, and the Hopi, in which brothers visit sisters. As Richards points out, this solution is applicable only where the population is rather large and compactly settled, so that men can move easily back and forth.

2. The fraternal extended family, in which brothers form the core, sending out sisters and bringing in wives.

3. The solution of the borrowed husband, or uxorilocality. The women form the core group, sending out brothers and bringing in husbands.

4. The solution of the selected heir, in which one or more boys of the matrilineage go to the mother's brother as coresidents and heirs, and the others remain with their father. This divides the children between the two categories of men who are most concerned with them, their fathers and their mothers' brothers.

Richards' paper is essentially concerned with the allocation of authority over the woman and her children between her husband and her brother. She relates this to other features of the society.

Nakane (1967) attempted a rather more ambitious typology of matrilineal social organization, based not only upon residence but also upon the inheritance of property. For four of the five types, she identifies a central core upon which the organization is based:

1. The Garo type, in which husband and wife form the central dyad and the daughter inherits the property;

2. The Nayar type, in which the siblings form the core group;

3. The Khasi type, in which the mother and daughter form the key dyad and depend upon either the brother or the husband;

4. The Ashanti type, in which the central dyad is the mother's brother and sister's son, and the man depends upon either his wife or his sister;

5. The Bemba type, in which the property group is not coterminous with the matrilineal descent group. (This type has the character of a residual category.)

A third typology of matrilineal social organization has been presented by Fox (1967). This is rather similar to that of Richards, in that he uses residence as his criterion. His four solutions to the matrilineal puzzle are: (a) to keep all members of the matrilineage together, with duolocal residence (b) to keep the males together, with avunculocal residence (c) to keep the females together, with matrilocal residence; and (d) to disperse all, with virilocal or neolocal residence.

No survey of the literature on matrilineal kinship would be complete without a discussion of the most important single work in that field, *Matrilineal Kinship* (Schneider and Gough 1961). This is a comprehensive examination of matrilineal societies, covering nine in detail and six more in the section on variations in matrilineal systems. In the latter section (Part II), Gough sets up a typology of matrilineal systems. Unlike those mentioned above, which focus on the internal workings of the society, Gough's typology is based upon the adaptation of the society to the external environment and the social consequences of these adaptations. She states:

My concern is to develop a rough classification of types of
ecology and types of over-all political organization and economic organization in matrilineal societies. I shall then enquire
into the implications of these over-all classifications for the
small-scale political and economic organizations of descent
groups, and also into their implications for other characteristics
of descent groups—for example, genealogical structure and local
distribution [Schneider and Gough 1961: 448].

For the purposes of this study, the most interesting sec-
tions of *Matrilineal Kinship* are Part III, "Cross-cultural
Comparisons," by David Aberle, and the Introduction, by
David Schneider. Aberle takes an evolutionary perspective.
He plots the distribution of matrilineal societies by geographical and ecological areas, and he compares matrilineal
societies with societies having other descent systems for
such adaptive mechanisms as subsistence type, size of political unit, and stratification. This is discussed further in
Chapter 2.

Schneider presents in the Introduction what he believes
to be general features of matrilineal descent systems. In dis-
cussing the allocation of authority over women and children, he makes the valuable contribution of distinguishing
clearly between the descent group and the domestic group.
He states:

> For our purposes only two spheres are immediately important:
> the domestic sphere and the descent-group sphere. It is suffi-
> cient, then, to define the male sex role as having authority over
> the statuses occupied by women within the context of each of
> these spheres. This means that men of the descent group have
> authority over the women and children of that descent group,
> that adult males of the domestic group have authority over the
> women and children of that domestic group [Schneider and
> Gough 1961: 7].

THE PROBLEM

Schneider's statement clarifies the distinction between
the descent group and the domestic group. In doing so, it
simplifies the problem of the matrilineal puzzle, for the implication of this statement is that authority in matrilineal
societies over women and children is always, to some ex-

tent, divided between the women's brothers in the descent group sphere and their husbands in the domestic group sphere (except, perhaps, for those rare cases of duolocal residence in which the groups are coterminous). We can take it for granted that authority in the descent group sphere is of necessity in the hands of the men of the matrilineage, the brothers and mothers' brothers of the women. What about authority in the domestic group sphere? Is Schneider's solution a true representation? It seems to be oversimplified, when we recall virilocal households in matrilineal societies, such as those of the Yao village headmen and the Trobiand Islanders, in which the woman residing in her husband's domestic group is still very much under the authority of her brother.

The problem, then, is the allocation of authority in the domestic group. Is there overlap between the husband and the brother of the woman? If so, to what degree?

This question of the interplay between brothers-in-law brought to mind the model put forward by Lévi-Strauss in his paper, "Structural Analysis in Linguistics and in Anthropology" (1963). In this model, the husband and brother are in opposition in relation to the woman who links them: in those societies in which the brother-sister dyad is characterized by "free and familiar relations," the husband-wife dyad is characterized by "hostility, antagonism, or reserve," and vice versa (Lévi-Strauss 1963: 44-45). It occurred to me to extract this concept of opposition between brothers-in-law from the Lévi-Strauss model, which was designed to illustrate the allocation of sentiment, and apply it to the allocation of authority within the domestic sphere.

Thinking along these lines of opposition between husband and brother, I assumed that if one of these key male figures, husband or brother, had greater authority over the adult married woman, the other, of course, would have less. By authority I mean the legitimate right to control the actions of another person. To brother authority versus husband authority I added a third possibility: the case in which authority, to whatever degree men actually do control women, is about equal; so that we cannot say for Society X that brothers have more control over adult sisters than husbands have over wives.

This suggested a gradient, from extreme brother control to extreme husband control. I constructed a model of five logically possible types:

1. Type I, strong husband authority;
2. Type II, husband authority tempered by brother authority in certain spheres;
3. Type III, equivalent brother and husband authority;
4. Type IV, strong brother authority with husband authority in certain spheres; and
5. Type V, strong brother authority. (See Figure 1.)

FIGURE 1: The Domestic Authority Gradient

Husband Authority . . . . Brother Authority

Type I	*Type II*	*Type III*	*Type IV*	*Type V*
Tiwi	Crow	Hopi	Khasi	North
	Plateau	Timbira	Truk	Kerala
	Tonga		Yao	Nayar
	Northern			
	Tuareg			

Having constructed the logical model, I looked for matrilineal societies which would fit the five focal points on the gradient. As this model was to be used for hypothesis construction, it was important to get as wide a representation as possible of different world areas, subsistence types, and levels of sociopolitical organization.

For strong husband authority, I selected the Tiwi, a society in which the husband has virtual right of life or death over the wife. For strong brother authority, I selected the North Kerala Nayar, where the duolocal household is under the control of the male lineage head and husbands only visit wives.

The selection of societies to fit Type II, husband authority tempered with some brother authority, and Type IV, brother authority tempered with some husband authority, was a little more difficult. When I constructed the model, I had not yet developed coding criteria for typological placement—one purpose of the model was to do so—and I had to rely upon intuition and general impressions to select the societies from which the criteria would be developed. I settled upon Crow, Plateau Tonga, and Northern Tuareg (Ahaggar drum group) as examples of societies in which control by the husband predominates over that by the brother, and Khasi, Truk, and Yao as examples of societies in which fraternal control of the woman is strong but not exclusive of husband authority. (After reading the literature on the remainder of the societies in this study, I am satisfied that my initial impressions were correct.)

Type III, in which neither husband nor brother exert greater control over the woman, is a type that I became acquainted with in my fieldwork on the Hopi reservation. I had gone to Hopiland assuming that brothers would exert a good deal of authority over the women, and husbands virtually none. What I saw, in fact, was a delicate balance of tactful suggestion and subtle pressure on the part of both, while the women actually "ruled the roost." The Hopi as they exist today, therefore, are ideal candidates for placement in Type III. Along with them, I placed the Timbira of Brazil, a somewhat similarly organized society.

The model, then, contains a variety of matrilineal societies. The world areas represented are Africa (Plateau Tonga, Tuareg, Yao), Asia (Khasi, Nayar), Oceania (Tiwi, Truk), North America (Crow, Hopi), and South America (Timbira). By subsistence type, there are hunter-gatherers (Tiwi), nomadic herders (Tuareg), intensive animal harvesters (Crow), horticulturalists (Hopi, Plateau Tonga, Timbira, Truk, and Yao), and advanced agriculturalists (Nayar). By sociopolitical level, they vary from band (Tiwi) on the one extreme to proto-state (Tuareg) and state (Nayar) on the other, the remainder falling within the "middle range" (Cohen, Schlegel, et al. 1968).

TWO THEOREMS

The model generates several important theoretical questions. It was from this model that the coding criteria for placement of societies on the authority gradient were developed, as well as the hypotheses to be tested. The questions I ask have to do with the relationship between the patterns of authority, as indicated by placement on the gradient, and features of both the domestic groups and the sociocultural milieu within which they exist. These are discussed in Chapter 2.

At this point I should like to present two theorems, or underlying hypotheses, upon which this work is based.

1. *The model is representative of domestic organization in matrilineal societies.* The model portrays a neat, logical gradient. What remains to be shown is that it is representative of the cluster of matrilineal societies. To do this, I shall have to present two kinds of evidence. First, I shall have to be able to code matrilineal societies into the five authority pattern categories. Second, I shall have to demonstrate that there are statistically significant associations between each of the authority patterns and a cluster of related traits. Only if I can do the latter can the authority types be said to be meaningful classes.

2. *As domestic power disperses, it declines.* In constructing the model, and in the discussion so far, I have deliberately avoided stating or implying that Type III domestic groups grant greater authority to women than do either husband authority or brother authority societies. There is no logical reason why this should be so: spheres of authority could conceivably be equally allocated to husband and brother without allowing for any margin of authority to accrue to the woman. What we see from the model, however, is societies in which women are not only free from differential authority of either husband or brother but also free from very much authority at all. For both the Hopi and the Timbira, the women own the houses, control the supply of domestic material goods, and participate freely and actively in the greater social life. This leads me to propose that in Type III societies there is not only lesser concentration of authority over women but also lesser authority.

TWO HYPOTHESES

Although I reserve a discussion of the hypotheses to be tested for the next chapter, there are two that emerge from the model that I consider to be the most important hypotheses of this study. For that reason, they are introduced now. Each will be discussed later, in Chapters 10 and 11.

Domestic Authority and Unilateral Cross-Cousin Marriage

The first is the hypothesis that there is covariation between the authority pattern and preference for one of the forms of unilateral cross-cousin marriage, either the matrilateral or the patrilateral form. I hypothesize that matrilateral cross-cousin marriage is associated with husband authority in the domestic group, and that patrilateral cross-cousin marriage is associated with brother authority in the domestic group. (See Figure 2.) Let us examine each one further.

FIGURE 2: Domestic Authority and Cross-Cousin Marriage

A: Matrilateral cross-cousin marriage, compatible with husband domestic authority: Ego brings his sister's son into the domestic group over which he has authority, his wife's.

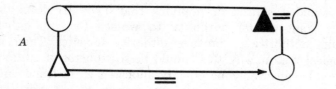

B: Patrilateral cross-cousin marriage, compatible with brother domestic authority: Ego brings his own son into the domestic group over which he has authority, his sister's.

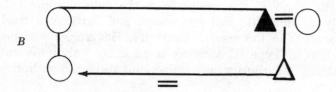

For societies of Type I and Type II, complete or partial husband authority, the husband has authority over the domestic group of his wife. Within the descent group sphere, he has authority over his sister's son. By means of matrilateral cross-cousin marriage, he brings his sister's son, the person over whom he has descent group control, into the domestic group of his wife, over which he has domestic group control.

For societies of Type IV and Type V, partial or complete brother authority, the brother has authority over the domestic group of his sister. He has no domestic group authority over his son, but he does have a strong interest in him, stemming from years of close association. By marrying his son to his sister's daughter, he incorporates the son into the group over which he, the father, has both descent group and domestic group authority.

Both forms of cross-cousin marriage unite the domestic group over which the adult man has control with the one in which he has a strong interest. In societies with husband authority over the domestic group, the adult man has an interest in his sister's domestic group, as that is where his closest descent group affiliations lie. In societies with brother authority over the domestic group, the adult man has a strong interest in his wife's domestic group. His ties to that group lie in the marital bond between himself and his wife and in the bond of nurture and affection toward his children. Thus the matrilineal puzzle of conflicting loyalties would be solved in the marital arrangements of the second generation through combining descent group and domestic group ties.

From the model there is weak evidence to support this hypothesis. In three cases in which there is preferential cross-cousin marriage, it is in the expected direction: the patrilateral form for Truk (Type IV) and the matrilateral form for the Tiwi and the Tuareg (Types I and II). The Nayar (Type V) deviate from this, with some preference for the matrilateral form; however, the conflict of loyalties is not so strong for this society—which suppresses ties to the wife and her children and emphasizes those to the sister and her children—as it is for other societies, which have a greater division of responsibility.

Domestic Authority and the Direction of the Incest Taboo

The second hypothesis to emerge from the model is that there is a difference in attitudes toward the incest taboo depending upon the authority pattern of the domestic group. This hypothesis states that in societies in which fraternal authority characterizes the domestic group, there will be an emphasis upon sibling incest; while in societies in which the husband has authority over the domestic group, the emphasis will be upon father-daughter incest. By emphasis, I mean that one form of incest will be regarded as more heinous or repulsive than the other, or will be followed by more severe natural or supernatural punishment. This is not to say that both forms will not be proscribed, but there are degrees of proscription, according to the relative evil of the feature under consideration. This hypothesis is derived from the strong contrast in attitudes toward incest between the Nayar and the Yao, on the brother authority end of the gradient, and the Crow and the Tiwi, on the husband authority end. For both the Nayar and the Yao, sibling incest is one of the worst crimes that can be committed. Father-daughter incest is repulsive, but it does not bring about the severe sanctions incurred by the other form. In contrast, Crow mythology presents father-daughter incest as "a most wicked thing," and the legendary figure who commits it is called a "ghost" and a "crazy one" (Lowie 1918: 41-43). In the literature I consulted on the Tiwi, there was no mention of father-daughter incest, but there is a Tiwi tale in which an incestuous sibling pair are portrayed in the light of romantic tragedy (Mountford 1958). While these indications from the mythology of the two societies are a good deal more tenuous than the data from the Nayar and the Yao, they do suggest the possibility of a contrast in attitudes between societies at either end of the domestic authority gradient. In addition, when I questioned Hopi informants on their attitude toward the two types of incest, these members of a Type III society replied that they were equally bad, that both were unthinkable, and that if anyone did such a thing "we would laugh at him." Therefore, I hypothesize that father-daughter incest will be emphasized in Type I and Type II societies and that sibling incest will be emphasized in Type IV and Type V societies. For Type III societies, I predict that either (a) both forms will be considered equally bad, or (b) there will be a random distribution of the two attitudes.

The method being used to test these and the other hypotheses is the cross-cultural method, first developed at the end of the last century. One of the pioneers in the systematic use of cross-cultural data was E. B. Tylor. In a famous address to the Royal Anthropological Institute of Great Britain and Ireland, Tylor showed statistical associations between various customs related to kin behavior (Tylor, as reprinted in Moore 1966). At about the same time, in Holland, Steinmetz was promoting the use of statistical techniques applied to data from a large number of societies (Köbben, as reprinted in Moore 1966). Under his leadership there developed a Dutch school, which produced a spurt of writings on general theoretical questions. By 1935, this burst of interest in cross-cultural research had more or less died out, and the single-case and concomitant variation types of studies were favored. Nevertheless, the ground was being prepared for the revival of this method on a much grander scale. In 1937, the Cross-cultural Survey was organized at the Institute of Human Relations, Yale University (Murdock, as reprinted in Moore 1966). In 1949, with the publication of Murdock's *Social Structure*, the potential of this method was brought strongly to the attention of anthropologists, and the revival was underway.

The cross-cultural method, as developed in recent years by Murdock, Driver, Naroll, Whiting and Child, and others, has as its aim the establishment of general laws or tendencies of human behavior. By using evidence garnered from societies widely dispersed through space and time and, where the problem requires it, at different levels of socioeconomic development, the attempt is made to control for variables having restricted distribution. That is to say, the generality of the laws and tendencies is established by constructing the sample from which evidence is taken as broadly as possible. This will be discussed further in Chapter 3. The procedure is to set up a null hypothesis, i.e. "X and Y are not associated." If, through the use of statistical techniques, the null hypothesis is rejected, then we have strong support for the argument that X and Y *are* functionally related. The advantage of this method is that, by statistically establishing laws or tendencies, it avoids the fruitless arguments that ensue when one or more cases contradict the tendency observed in other cases. The cross-cultural method allows for deviant cases: it assumes a multiplicity of factors working to produce functional associations—with the possibilities that in some cases some of these factors may be absent or that other features in the society will override or qualify the factors which, otherwise, might have produced the presence of the associated traits in that society. Through the use of statistical techniques, the functional association of two or more traits can be established cross-culturally, and a statement about the general nature of this association can be made. The generality of the statement, of course, depends upon the problem under investigation and the representativeness of the sample used.

For the present study, the hypotheses to be tested and the statements to be made apply to the universe of matrilineal societies. In the following chapters, I discuss the hypotheses derived from consideration of the model and the method and techniques employed to test them.

Theoretical Considerations

In the preceding chapter we examined five types of matrilineal domestic organization. What are the conditions that give rise to these types? What are the consequences of these authority patterns for interpersonal rules and relationships within the domestic group?

To provide a theoretical framework for a testing plan, we can look at the problem from the point of view of the system. The advantage in the systems approach is that one need not worry about immediate cause and effect, although one can often distinguish logically or historically antecedent and consequent variables; one simply assumes that there is feedback within the system to a greater or lesser degree. The systems approach thus provides greater flexibility than the linear, causal approach, for one can expand or contract the number and kinds of variables according to which seem most pertinent to the problem, without tacitly implying that other variables might not also be contributing to the effect.

In this study, I am regarding the authority pattern as the intervening variable between factors in the society outside the domestic group and the responses within it.[1] In terms of systems theory, I have looked at features in the society

[1] This approach is somewhat similar to that of Hsu (1965), in his work on dominant dyads. He sees the dominant dyad as the intervening variable between the society (the input) and the family (the output), and the family pattern as itself the mechanism by which society and culture are maintained.

at large as inputs and features of the domestic group as outputs. The outputs themselves can feed back into the system as inputs, either by acting directly upon the authority pattern or by acting upon the societal inputs. For example, I have taken subsistence techniques to be inputs, features that affect the authority pattern. While it would be difficult to imagine what possible effect the presence of such a domestic group custom as bride capture might have upon the subsistence techniques, one can readily suppose that other domestic group features, such as allocation of control over property or the residence pattern, and their consequences for the organization of labor, might well be determining factors in the development and perpetuation of subsistence techniques. On the other hand, the custom of bride capture could be thought of as working directly upon the authority pattern, for it could be seen as a means of establishing at the outset of the marriage the husband's control over the wife, by force if necessary.

However, I am not immediately concerned with the feedbacks in this study. My problems are to account for the domestic authority pattern and to discuss the kinds of rules and relationships one finds associated with each type. Since this study focuses on the nature of the domestic group in the society and culture, the inputs are less important to it and therefore receive less attention. (See Figure 3.)

FIGURE 3: The Domestic Authority System

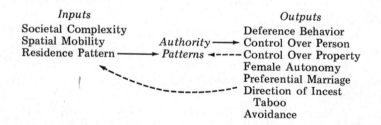

Inputs		Outputs
Societal Complexity		Deference Behavior
Spatial Mobility	Authority ⟶	Control Over Person
Residence Pattern ⟶	Patterns ◄----	Control Over Property
		Female Autonomy
		Preferential Marriage
		Direction of Incest Taboo
		Avoidance

INPUTS

Societal Complexity

From the model we can see that a variety of economic, political, and stratification systems coexist with the different authority types. In a general way, the model shows a gradation from the most complex society, on the brother authority end of the continuum, to the least, the Tiwi, on the husband authority end—with the exception of the Tuareg, a literate and politically well-organized society. However, this may be an artifact of the model.

From the study done by Aberle (1961) we can get an idea of how matrilineal societies compare with those having other descent systems. I will briefly review Aberle's findings here. He had a sample of 84 matrilineal societies, chosen from the "World Ethnographic Sample" (Murdock 1957).

Comparing societies by productivity, it is clear that the majority of matrilineal societies are horticultural: 68 percent of matrilineal societies as compared to 47 percent of all societies in the "World Ethnographic Sample." Pastoralism is underrepresented among matrilineal societies—6 percent compared to 14 percent, as is plow agriculture—11 percent compared to 21 percent. There is little difference in extractive societies—16 percent compared to 18 percent.

Looking at political integration, the majority of matrilineal societies fall into the "middle range" (Cohen, Schlegel, et al. 1968). Thirty-two percent of matrilineal societies fall into the "minimal states" level (which seems to be mostly chiefdoms), compared with 21 percent of all societies. The greatest difference lies in the "states" level—1 percent compared with 14 percent of all. A similar pattern emerges when one regards social stratification: hereditary stratification is represented by 28 percent among matrilineal societies, compared to 21 percent of all, and complex stratification is at 7 percent, compared to 18 percent.

We can see from this brief résumé that matrilineality as a system of reckoning descent is associated with certain levels of social complexity. Aberle's concern was with the descent principle. Mine is with the domestic group; and I shall examine the different types of authority patterns to see whether associations exist between authority types and societal features.

I have selected four features of economic life as indexes of productivity. (For coding criteria, see Chapter 4.) These are: intensity of agriculture, intensity of animal use, presence or absence of economic orientation toward trade, and degree of craft specialization. I am assuming that the more intensive the agriculture, the higher the energy utilization, i.e. the more the food output per individual producer. Protein in the form of domesticated animals is assumed to be more conservative of human energy than protein in the form of hunting or fishing. However, there are exceptions: a society with sophisticated extractive techniques and very rich resources is likely to get as high a level of protein with as little expenditure of human energy as a society keeping domesticated animals. In this study I consider the intensive use of nondomesticated animals to be equivalent to herding as a means of supplying protein. Strong trade orientation implies an excess of produced goods beyond immediate needs. Degree of craft specialization also implies a prior surplus, as full-time specialists cannot exist where every man is primarily a food producer.

I am testing political integration to see whether there is any association between organization of power and authority in the society at large and in the domestic group.

I am testing social stratification to see whether hierarchy in the domestic group—authority of husband or brother over the woman—is consonant with hierarchy in the society.

Spatial Mobility

Another feature that emerges from the model is the seeming association between domestic authority pattern and spatial mobility. The Nayar are the least mobile and the Tiwi are the most. Those societies which have been classified as having husband authority are all more mobile than the others: the Crow are equestrian hunters, the Tuareg are

nomadic herders, and the Plateau Tonga are shifting agriculturalists. There is not a clear gradient, however, as the Hopi
are no more mobile than societies in Type II. The association needs to be examined, using the larger sample.

Residence Pattern

Residence pattern is a feature of community organization
quite clearly associated with authority pattern in the model. The Nayar are duolocal. Type II and Type III societies
are matrilocal. Type IV and Type V societies are virilocal.

Most authorities agree on the importance of residence
pattern to domestic organization. Richards states: "In all
these forms of family structure the crucial point, I have
suggested, is the question of residence at marriage" (Richards 1950: 249). Gough suggests that a shift to patrilocal
residence precedes a shift to patrilineal descent (Gough
1961b: 565). Both Nakane (1967) and Fox (1967: 112-13)
base matrilineal family organization type upon residence
pattern. The association is not perfect, however; the Siriono
(not in the model) have matrilocal residence and strong
husband authority, and the wife of a Yao warden is under
ultimate control of her brothers even though she may be
living virilocally. This leads me to propose that the association between residence type and authority pattern is not
tautological and merits testing.

OUTPUTS

I give the term *outputs* to those sociocultural variables
which can be thought of as consequences of the domestic
authority pattern. The variables that follow are so closely
associated with the authority pattern as to be, perhaps, better considered as aspects of it. However, as we shall see,
there are very few tautological associations. The variables
under discussion here can be perused in the Coding Manual
(Appendix A) under "I: Coding for Typological Placement." Within this group, I consider three kinds of variables: deference behavior, control over person, and control
over property.

Deference Behavior

Stephens presents a discussion of deference as it relates to family behavior (Stephens 1963: 291 ff., chap. 7). Deference is a means of indicating differential status. Stephens maintains that it indicates differential power as well: "A deference custom . . . is a ritual expression or cultural expectation of an unequal power relationship" (Stephens 1963: 296). This is not, I believe, always the case. It would be difficult to imagine the elaborate deference toward women in upper-class Western society of the last century as a mark of female power, in spite of the fact that the postural and positional attitudes of men vis-à-vis women were similar to those exhibited by subordinates to superiors in same-sex relationships, e.g. clerk to employer or junior to senior officer. Nor is power always indicated by deference: Hopi women rule the home, and yet I was never able to distinguish any male to female deference, either within the home or in public.

The model only partially supports the association of deference and authority. Among the Nayar, women defer to both brother and husband. In the Type IV societies, deference of sister to brother is reported only for Truk, none is reported for Yao, and among the Khasi the wife defers to her husband. No deference is reported for either Hopi or Timbira. For all of the Type II and I societies, however, wife to husband deference is reported, and none of these is reported to have sister to brother deference. Perhaps it is wiser to take the more conservative view that deference is indicative of status differential, which may or may not be correlated with authority. I take deference as a variable to see how, and to what degree, status differential within the domestic group corresponds to authority patterns.

Control Over Person

The variables in this category, and the reasons for choosing them, are explained in the Coding Manual. The only one that demands additional comment here is the cluster of variables regarding marriage payment.

I have divided bridewealth and bride service into two types, substantial and token. While it is possible that the latter may be more of a gift than a compensation, I consider the former to be payment in some form for the woman. Since children do not belong to the husband and his kin group in matrilineal societies, it is rights over the woman that are being transferred (although some rights over minor children must also be considered). A number of societies are quite explicit about just what these rights are: "We pay for her genitals," or an equivalent expression, appears with some frequency in the ethnographies.

It is reasonable to suppose that the greater the degree of control of husband over wife, in sexual and other matters, the higher the bridewealth in proportion to the wealth of the society. I hypothesize that substantial bridewealth will be found more often in societies with husband authority, and that token bridewealth, or none, will be found in the other types.

Bride service is a form of bridewealth, giving labor instead of goods. I have chosen six months as the marker between token and substantial bride service. Six months may seem a long time for token service, but it is to be remembered that the new husband is supporting himself and his wife, so that only a part of his labor is going for the benefit of his affines.

I propose that woman exchange is the highest possible form of bridewealth, as an exact equivalent is given for the woman received. I hypothesize, therefore, that woman exchange is found in association with strong husband control. (I was led to this idea both by logic and by considering the practices of the Tiwi, an example of strong husband authority, who are substituting bridewealth and bride service for the traditional custom of woman exchange. I later discovered that Ronhaar had also come to the same conclusion [Ronhaar 1931: 394-95].)

The societies in the model fit this pattern. There is no bridewealth among the Nayar, nor is there any for Types IV and III. Substantial bridewealth is reported for all societies of Type II. For the Tiwi, Type I, woman exchange is the traditional form, which is today being replaced with high bride-price and high bride service.

Control over Property

Here also the Coding Manual gives an explanation of the different forms of property control. The hypothesis is that control is associated with authority; so that husband or brother control correspond with husband or brother authority, and Type III is associated with some form of partial or total female control.

A gradient is seen in the societies that comprise the model. The brother who is head of the household has complete control over domestic group property among the Nayar. The brother has a lesser degree of control over property among the Truk, Khasi, and Yao, where some of the wife's labor goes to benefit her husband. Among the Hopi and the Timbira, the women own the houses and household goods and control all or much of the land used by their husbands. In the societies of Type II, the husbands control most of the group property, although in each case women have some property rights going beyond personal articles. Among the Tiwi, where property is at a minimum, it appears that the husband controls the food supply, which is the only common domestic group property I could discover.

The following output variables are those which are less directly associated with the domestic authority pattern than the preceding ones. The posited association may be logical, as, for example, avoidance rules and authority patterns; or it may be derived from current assumptions, such as the assumed association between female subordination and menstrual restrictions; or it may have emerged from the model, as is the case with domestic authority and the direction of the incest taboo. These variables can be examined in detail in Part II of the Coding Manual.

Degree of Female Autonomy

I have examined a cluster of traits which have been thought to be associated with the status of women in and out of the home. I have chosen the term *female autonomy* rather than *status of women*, as I feel that the latter is misleading, in that it overlooks the functional differences of the sex roles and defines female activities in relation to male activities—i.e. the more women can participate in activities performed by men, the higher their status is. It is perfectly obvious that at all times and places most women center their activities around the domestic sphere, and most men either center their activities around a communitywide or societywide sphere or use the domestic group as an economically and socially productive unit. It is also obvious that this is functional when most women spend most of their adult lives pregnant, nursing, or caring for children.

Female autonomy, as I use it, does not refer to women's equivalence to men but rather to a woman's control over her person and activities and her meaningful contribution to society beyond breeding and feeding.

Plural marriage. Loeb expresses a commonly held sentiment when he states: "The usual effect of polygyny is, obviously, to depress the position of women" (Loeb 1962: 137). I have selected variables relating to plural marriage to see whether this notion can be confirmed. I distinguish between limited and general polygyny on the grounds that limited polygyny may be more of a status marker for men (high status for the few polygynists) than for women (low status because of enforced competition). Given polygyny, it becomes necessary to distinguish between the sororal and nonsororal forms: I hypothesize that sororal polygyny enhances female autonomy, as I see sisters presenting a united front that elevates all. With nonsororal polygyny, are co-wives believed to be jealous of each other? I hypothesize that co-wife jealousy is associated with husband authority, as wives compete for access to the center of power in the home. Finally, how does polyandry fit in? I hypothesize that it is negatively associated with husband dominance, as the common wife can play one husband against the other.

Sexual restrictions. A woman's right to dispose of her sexuality might be taken as a measure of her personal autonomy, as might adultery regulations which weigh equally upon husband and wife. We can expect a double standard to prevail in societies in which the husband is dominant, and a more lenient attitude toward wife's adultery to be found with other authority patterns.

Social positions. This group of variables asks about the right of women to hold positions of importance in the society outside the home. If I were redoing this study, I would also ask the number, as well as the kinds, of positions women might hold, as there is considerable variation in this respect. I hypothesize that participation in many kinds of positions corresponds with Type III. A question on the public performance of women has been included to determine whether there is any association between general female participation in public social activities and type of authority pattern.

Menstrual restrictions. Menstrual restrictions are widespread and have an effect upon the rhythm of relations between the sexes, particularly within the domestic group, wherever they occur. At the least, the loss of the wife as a sexual object, and perhaps as cook or household worker, may cause annoyance to the husband, particularly in monogamous families. Many societies see menstruating women as dangerous to men, to sacred objects, and even to crops or livestock, so that in these societies there is the added inconvenience of watching the menstruating women so that they do not inadvertently cause mischief.

Menstrual restrictions have received considerable attention, particularly by scholars interested in sexual customs (Frazer 1907-27) or psychoanalytic explanations of culture (Bettelheim 1962; Devereux 1950). To my knowledge, there are four systematic investigations of these restrictions cross-culturally. The first in time, by Ford, advances the hypotheses that menstrual restrictions are consequences of disgust at elimination, and/or absence of menstrual pads (Ford 1945). Stephens (1962) disconfirms these. In an elaborate study, he presents associations between the strength of menstrual restrictions and factors which might lead to the Oedipal complex, the complex itself being regarded as the intervening, but untested, variable. His sample includes six matrilineal societies. (I do not count the Ainu as matrilineal, for reasons given below, p. 31.) If we agree that his antecedent variables do in fact measure castration anxiety, and that castration anxiety is expressed in restrictions on menstruating women, then his hypotheses have been confirmed. (This study incorporates and expands upon Stephens, 1961.) This is not the place for a detailed criticism, but I feel that there are too many untested assumptions for the hypotheses, and the findings, to be completely satisfactory.

Young and Bacdayan (1965) also take up the question. Assuming that menstrual taboos are discriminatory against women, they attempt to find correlates with other features of societal organization. They find a statistically significant association with a feature they call "social rigidity," or the "relative lack of intercommunication among the parts of the system" (Young and Bacdayan: 230-31). They also find (p. 232) a significant association between social rigidity and male dominance, measured by male solidarity (itself measured by the presence of certain cultural traits), exogamy, banishment, and the levirate. (Surely this is the long way around: I was able to get what I feel to be satisfactory data on male dominance by looking for statements about it.) They consider menstrual taboos and male dominance to be related as aspects of the same societal feature, social rigidity.

Bock (1967) believes that geographic distribution accounts for Young and Bacdayan's associations. He also disagrees with their assumption that menstrual taboos discriminate against women: he mentions the claim put forth by Devereux (1950) that these taboos actually mark their superior status.

All of the persons mentioned so far, with the exception of Bock, assume that menstrual restrictions exist to set off in a direct way the status of woman. For most, this is assumed to be inferior to that of man. They forget that it is men who suffer as much or more from these restrictions: the menstrual hut, or a restriction on housework, might come as a welcome monthly vacation to the woman. Nevertheless, it is the women who are the focus of these restrictions, as they are the ones who bleed.

For the purpose of this study, I shall follow the convention and hypothesize that menstrual restrictions are associated with the status of women; i.e. that menstrual restrictions are more severe in Types I and II and/or IV and V than in Type III societies.

Preferential Marriage and Sibling Incest

These variables have been discussed in Chapter 1.

Avoidance

Intersex avoidance is often taken to be a broadening of incest taboos. This has been made explicit by Stephens and D'Andrade (1962), who consider avoidances to be the result of displaced sexual desire for persons tabooed by the incest restrictions. According to them, mothers, sisters, and daughters are desired sexual objects. Mothers and daughters are so strongly tabooed that a phobic reaction sets in and there is no need to avoid them. (While it is probably true that mothers are never avoided, Stephens and D'Andrade [1962: 128] are wrong when they claim that daughters are not.) The incestuous feelings are then displaced toward mother-in-law and daughter-in-law, and to prevent the acting out of such impulses, these persons are avoided. The authors do not explain why sisters are so often avoided: being themselves products of a culture in which sibling incest is not so heinous as either form of parent-child incest, it is possible that they felt no need to assume a phobic reaction to incestuous feelings toward the sister as they did toward mother or daughter.

In this study I am not concerned with affines and displacements: my concern is with the two kinds of avoidance behavior that might be the results of differential authority patterns. I propose two alternative hypotheses:

1. Sibling avoidance occurs most frequently in societies with husband authority, as a mechanism for keeping the brother, who has some authority over his sister within the descent group, from interfering in her marriage, in which her husband has authority. This hypothesis has nothing to say about father-daughter avoidance.

2. Sibling avoidance and father-daughter avoidance are extensions of incest taboos. If, as I have hypothesized in the preceding chapter, greater concern over sibling incest is a response to the brother authority pattern and greater concern with the father-daughter form is associated with the husband authority pattern, then we would expect the avoidance regulations also to be so associated.

In this chapter I have presented the features which, it seemed to me, might be related to the domestic authority pattern. They have been divided into two sets: inputs, or features of the greater society which might have an effect upon the nature of domestic power relationships, and outputs, or features of family life and kinship organization which might be conditioned by these power relationships.

By arranging the traits to be tested in this manner, I have emphasized the concept of the domestic group as central to the larger system of social relationships. In this, my ideas closely parallel those of Hsu (1965). Hsu, however, looks at the system through time, and one of his major hypotheses is that the emotional organization of the family —he treats dyadic relationships in terms of emotions, attitudes, and values—is an important, if not the most important, socializing agent, which produces personalities that respond to and create their culture and society according to patterns already set by their early domestic experiences. My approach is not so complex. First, for purposes of analysis, it is synchronic. (Of course, movement through time is implicit in the concept of the system, but this study does not specifically handle this question.) Second, I am treating only four of the possible dyadic relationships in domestic organization: husband/wife and brother/sister in some detail, and father/daughter and the brother-in-law relationship cursorily. Third, I am only concerned with one kind of relationship, power, and some of the affects, attitudes, and overt behavior associated with it. The rich fabric of dyadic affects, including those threads of love, support, need for approval, resentment, and all the rest that make up the whole cloth, I leave to other, more psychologically complex, treatments.

3

Sampling

Of all the pitfalls which the unwary cross-cultural researcher may encounter, probably the one which casts greatest doubt upon the reliability of his findings is improper sample construction.

It would appear, on first glance, that the ideal way of conducting a cross-cultural test would be to utilize the entire universe, or close to it, of described societies—such as those collected in the Human Relations Area Files—excluding only those for which there is not enough data to test the problem. This would indeed eliminate the need for constructing a sample. However, it would entail the problem, first stated by Galton in 1889, of deciding when a society is an individual cultural entity and when it is a subunit of a larger cultural entity (Tylor 1966: 23). An example would be the unity or separability of Mandan, Crow, and Hidatsa societies. They are known from linguistic and cultural evidence to have diverged in fairly recent times. Are they to be considered three separate cultures or three societal subunits of a single culture? This problem would become acute if one took, for example, China as a single case and the hundreds of similar but individually named and ethnically self-conscious Australian bands as multiple cases. Murdock discusses this in his explanation of the "World Ethnographic Sample" (Murdock 1966b: 196).

Another difficulty is that using the total universe is too unwieldy and time-consuming for most studies, which therefore depend upon a sample. The purpose of a sample, of course, is to select a number of cases which are representative of the total universe of cases to which the results of the study apply. Statistical purists insist that a sample be totally random, on the grounds that statistical tests of significance are not appropriate with other kinds of samples. This means that the sample has to be selected by means of a random numbers table, or some other device, to ensure that there is no possible way in which bias could enter sample construction and that every case in the universe of cases has an equal chance of being selected (Ember 1963: 234-35). (However, on this point see Naroll 1970: 1230.) A difficulty arises in that, if one selects entirely randomly from the universe of described societies, one is still left with Galton's problem. The solution Murdock suggests, and the one he applied in constructing the "World Ethnographic Sample," a sample of 565 cultures coded for 15 traits, is: (a) to stratify geographically, so that no world area or culture area is over- or underrepresented (i.e. one would have as great a chance of including China in the sample as any of the Australian bands); and (b) to avoid including duplicate cases by not selecting two societies from the same area that are geographically contiguous or characterized by mutually intelligible languages. Murdock qualifies this last restriction by adding: "unless they reveal such major differences in either their basic economy, their social organization, or in the former instance their languages, as to assure that they have achieved independent integration" (Murdock 1966b: 198).

To enable the reader to see the difference between a well-selected sample and one that is poorly selected, I shall compare Ember 1963 with Murdock 1949 and Cohen, Schlegel, et al. 1968. Ember drew his sample of 24 cases from Murdock's "World Ethnographic Sample" by means of a random numbers table. Because the nature of the study required politically autonomous cases, those societies which were subunits of larger societies and those with inadequate data were discarded and substitutes drawn randomly by the same procedure until the entire sample of 24 cases was achieved. One might question the very small size of this sample as leading to the possibility that random error would have a skewing effect that would be counterbalanced in a larger sample; but that does not detract from the correctness of his selection procedure.

Murdock cites his own book, *Social Structure* (1949) as an example of poor sample selection (Murdock 1967: 3). He notes some examples of duplicate cases, and states that several categories of known and adequately described societies were unrepresented. As for Cohen and Schlegel's study, we selected a sample to be geographically stratified and representative of the variety of political and subsistence types within middle-range societies. While this could be a pilot study for a larger research project, we were unwarranted in assuming that our results applied to the universe of middle-range societies.

Even though there were several important cross-cultural studies using large numbers of societies and sophisticated techniques of data collection and analysis before 1957 (e.g. Murdock 1949, Whiting and Child 1953), a look at any bibliography of cross-cultural research (e.g. Naroll 1970) will convince the reader that the appearance of Murdock's "World Ethnographic Sample" in that year created a tremendous stimulus to this kind of study. Cross-cultural research was further facilitated by the publication of the *Ethnographic Atlas*, begun in 1962 as installments in *Ethnology* and published in compact form in 1967 (Murdock 1967). In this work, the author constructs a quasi-universe of 862 well-described societies and divides them into 412 culture clusters. These are composed of societies which had a common origin less than 1,000 years ago, as determined by historical, linguistic, or ethnographic evidence (Murdock 1967: 3-4). A third work by Murdock which facilitates cross-cultural research is "World Sampling Provinces" (Murdock 1968). In this he groups culture clusters into 200 geographic sampling provinces. He makes the point that the need in cross-cultural research is for " 'stratified' samples carefully adapted to the facts of ethnographic variation and distribution" (Murdock 1968: 305). In each case in which there are more than one matrilineal societies, there is a "preferred" matrilineal society. Where the preferred society is not the sole matrilineal one in the province, Murdock does not give the criteria for selecting the preferred one out of the available ones. Judging from my own survey of the literature, these criteria appear to be the extensiveness and presumed reliability of the data.

The sample I selected for this study had to satisfy three criteria: it had to be large enough to meet the requirements for statistical tests of association; it had to avoid Galton's problem; and it had to be geographically representative. (Obviously, it had to include only matrilineal societies, which precluded the use of a standard ethnographic sample such as that prepared by Naroll et al., 1970.) The third feature is particularly important, as matrilineal societies tend to cluster geographically (e.g. the "matrilineal belt" of Africa), and their limited number relative to the universe of reported societies makes it probable that random selection would introduce a geographic bias.

My initial intention had been to use the 53 preferred matrilineal societies as the sample. This would have satisfied the criterion of geographic representation and reduced the likelihood of hyperdiffusional correlations (see below, Chapter 4). Under conditions of ideal reportage, that is of adequate data for each society, this would also have just met the first criterion, for sample size. However, when I began to code, it became apparent that the paucity of data for a number of the preferred societies would have resulted in a small and spotty sample. While a few sampling provinces might have several matrilineal societies well reported, others might have only one, and that one poorly covered. Therefore, I expanded the sample to include one society for each of the culture clusters that include one or more matrilineal societies, a total of 73 as coded in the *Ethnographic Atlas*. Out of these I discarded two, the Ainu and Rotuma. A recent report indicates that, while they may have a matrilineal tendency, the Ainu are bilateral (Suguru and Befu 1962). From the description of the Rotuma kinship system given by Gardiner (1898: 478, 484-85), I con-

sider them to be ambilineal. I added the Siriono, classified
by Murdock as bilateral, on the authority of Holmberg, the
major source of information on this society (Holmberg
1950: 50).

This created a potential sample of 72 matrilineal societies. Six of these were not used in the final sample. For
the Ami, the Serer, the Bijogo, and the Mimika, I was unable to get enough information to make coding worthwhile.
The two remaining societies, the Navajo and Cherokee,
were to be coded by ethnographers with field experience in
those societies. Neither of them got their codings to me in
time for inclusion in the study.[1]

The actual selection of societies from each sample was
based, in all cases but one, on the quantity and presumed
reliability of data. For all but two of the sampling provinces with preferred matrilineal societies, I accepted Murdock's choice. The two exceptions are Upper Missouri, in
which I substituted the Crow for the Mandan, and Pueblo-
Navajo, in which I substituted one Western Pueblo society,
Hopi, for the preferred one, Zuni. The former substitution
was made to include a full-blown Plains society in the sample, whereas there were other North American horticultural
societies similar to the Mandan in the sample. This substitution also expanded the number of societies depending upon
domesticated animals for maintenance of the economy (the
others being Tuareg and Goajiro). The latter substitution
was made because I am very familiar with the Hopi data,
having done fieldwork there. It is true that Murdock cau-
tions against using societies because one is familiar with
them (Murdock 1967: 5); however, for my purposes Hopi

[1] How would the findings have differed had these societies been
included? For the first four, I cannot say. For Cherokee and Navajo,
I speculate—on the basis of my own knowledge and informal conver-
sations with the ethnographers—that the association of Neither Dominant and Shared Control over Children with North America would
have been strengthened (both); there would have been another case
of bridewealth associated with Neither Dominant (Navajo), and
Navajo would have provided an exception to the association between
Intensive Use of Domesticated Animals and Husband Dominant (true
for Tuareg, Goajiro, and Crow).

is the best-described society in this province. For the remaining culture clusters, I selected the society for which there appeared to be the most extensive data, particularly that pertaining to kinship and family life.

If we accept Murdock's contention that each culture cluster (with a few minor qualifications) represents a single culture, of which the societies within it are subcultures, then this sample approaches being a total sample of the universe of matrilineal cultures. To have selected more than one society from any one cluster would have been to invite Galton's problem. The reader might point out that my selection of societies within culture clusters was not random when there was more than one matrilineal society represented, but I would counter that criticism with the need for as complete information as possible in a study that must rely on a limited number of cases. I am satisfied that it is representative of the universe of adequately described matrilineal cultures as of 1967. The reader may wish, however, to accept the findings only as they relate to each of the authority patterns to be discussed, rather than to matrilineality per se.

It is important in cross-cultural research to define the sampling unit, since one sort of unit—such as the worldwide community of believers in a religious doctrine—may be suitable for one type of study but not another. There is a growing body of literature on the nature and type of the sampling unit (Bessac 1968; Moerman 1965, 1968; Naroll 1964, 1967, 1968).

Each unit in this study was chosen from Murdock's *Ethnographic Atlas.* Murdock refers to these units as "societies," which term, however, does not clarify the nature of the unit; as a "society" may be a territorial-language group (Hopi), a political association (Iroquois), or a caste (Nayar).

Each of the units in the sample occupies a single delimited territory and shares a common language and culture, or "blueprint for living" (Naroll 1964: 288). We can classify these units into three kinds of groups:

1. The compact group. This is a group made up of one or a few villages or bands or a small island, which consti-

tutes or is representative of the entire territorial-language group. This is by far the most common type, as most ethnographers do their fieldwork in one or at most a few such compact groups. Where the compact group constitutes the entire territorial-language group, we can say that "the Wumpawumpa do thus and such." Where, however, the compact group is only one of many, we can only say with certainty that "the Wumpawumpa of X village/band/island do thus and such." For the purposes of cross-cultural sampling, this is not important, as we are comparing "blueprints" and not necessarily entire territorial-language groups.

2. The territorial-language group. It is sometimes impossible to know or infer that the ethnographer worked in a restricted geographical area, and in some cases, such as survey reports or travelers' accounts, it is known that he did not. In such instances we can only generalize the data to the entire territorial-language group. This group is often referred to in the literature as a "tribe." When the "tribe" is small and localized, such as the Tlingit, one can assume that references to "Tlingit culture" probably encompass the majority of Tlingit communities. We are on less certain grounds with larger territorial-language groups, such as the Fur of Darfur. The following are units in this study that cannot be pinpointed to a restricted set of communities, so that the data must be assumed to apply to the larger territorial-language group: Belu, Darfur, Goajiro, Kunama, Longudu, Luguru, and Saramacca.

3. Subcultural unit. The ethnographer states, or we can infer, that the unit to which his findings apply is a category of people within a territorial-language group. I give the following examples from this study:

a. Rattray applies his findings to late nineteenth/early twentieth-century Ashanti, but from his discussions it appears that his informants were members of the royal family and the upper class. We are safest if we take this to be the case, rather than generalize his data to all of Ashanti.

b. The same can be said for Loeb's discussion on Minangkabau: his references seem to be to at least substantial property owners.

c. The Nayar are a special case, a matrilineal caste group within a generally patrilineal caste hierarchy. Gough further restricts her findings to the upper castes of this caste group.

d. The Vedda are a language group divided into subgroups at various stages of incorporation into Ceylonese culture. The Seligmans discuss all the varieties of Vedda. I have limited my coding to the data on the "wild" Vedda. The data are less than satisfactory, as one datum comes from one band, another from another, and so forth.

The cross-cultural researcher must specify the time period to which his information refers, as well as the territorial boundaries. This can be confusing, as the coder may have access to ethnographies written at different times, or the ethnographer may mix into his accounts of the present attempted reconstructions of the past.

In Appendix B, the Coding Bibliography, I present the time period to which the codings apply. This can be either the date of the field trip—if the ethnographer relates conditions as they existed at the time of his visit—or it can be his reconstruction of the past, based primarily on the memories of aged informants.

A special problem arises in the use of distant historical reconstruction. There are three examples of this in the sample. The culture of the Delaware, a small localized language-political unit, has been reconstructed as it probably was in the eighteenth century. The Guanche of Tenerife in the Canaries are presented as they existed before Spanish conquest, or circa 1500. The culture of the Locono of the island of Hispaniola is reconstructed to its pre-Columbian antecedents. If many such cases were used in a study, some form of quality control test would have to be applied to ensure that possibly faulty reconstruction did not bias the data.

To summarize: the sample is, I believe, representative of the universe of matrilineal culture. It was selected to be geographically representative and at the same time to avoid Galton's problem. While the sampling units are not all strictly comparable in terms of size, compactness, or intensity of communication (i.e. we assume that there is more constant communication within a compact group than within a territorial-language group), they are comparable in that they are all "blueprints for living." The concern here is not with the statistical model—what people do at any given time—but rather with the theoretical model—what people say they do or should do.

4

Coding

DATA FROM PRIMARY SOURCES

Murdock et al. (1962-) give one or more sources of
information for each of the societies in the sample. In
many cases there are additional sources. I used all of the
sources in English, French, and German that were available
to me through local libraries and the Inter-Library Loan
system. In the Coding Bibliography, Appendix B, I indicate
the sources used in order of importance to this work and
the page references for each of the coding decisions. As a
final-step check, I consulted the Human Relations Area
Files at the University of Chicago in the attempt to eliminate "no information" codings for societies represented in
the Files. I found them particularly useful for their trans-
lations of works in Spanish and Portuguese dealing with
South American societies, works which are not widely
represented in the United States.

The coding manual, Appendix A, gives the coding instructions. Ideally, this should be entirely self-explanatory,
so that all intelligent coders with some experience with
ethnographic data should always make the same coding
decisions. In reality, this degree of perfection is rarely, if
ever, reached. I tested the manual with a class of junior and
senior undergraduate students majoring in anthropology.
The very best students coded satisfactorily, but the others
either did not understand the instructions or were careless
in marking down their decisions, and their code sheets had

to be discarded. Subsequently, I gained the assistance of a capable graduate student, who then coded most of the societies as my cocoder. The need for coder training was not so great in his case as it would have been with the undergraduate students, although there was an improvement in agreement between us as the work progressed. We did not discuss the hypotheses to be tested. Societies reported in German were cocoded by a native German speaker. I give the information on coder agreement in the chapter on trustworthiness.

Seven societies were coded by me alone, because I had coded them while away from home, and the material would not have reached us in time for my cocoder to use it. These societies are: Aua, Callinago, Dieri, Khasi, Lakalai, Locono, and Minangkabau. In addition, I had to discard the student coding on Tiwi, Truk, Tuareg, Yao, and Siriono. Four additional societies—Bororo, Coniagui, Lobi, and Mnong Gar—were coded by me alone, because the only or main source of data is in French. Hopi was coded by me alone, since I functioned in this case as the ethnographer, and any error here would be ethnographer's error rather than coder's error. William Davenport, the ethnographer, was gracious enough to code Santa Cruz. There are 16 societies, or 24 percent, then, which have no check on coder error.

The reader can refer to the coding manual for coding instructions. In addition to the instructions given there, I found myself coding according to the following procedures, and I trained my cocoders to do the same:

1. A trait is coded present or absent when there is a statement to that effect in the ethnography;

2. A trait is coded present when the presence of another trait necessitates it. For example, if we are told that women eat separately from men, then we code "present" for wife-to-husband deference, even though the specific husband-wife separation is not mentioned;

3. A trait is coded absent when the presence of another trait precludes it. For example, Callinago father-daughter and brother-sister avoidance were coded absent because

there are known cases of tolerated incestuous unions of these two types;

4. A trait is coded absent when there is a detailed discussion of the area in which it would occur which fails to mention it. For example, discussions on weddings and marriage which fail to mention bride capture or polyandry are taken to indicate their absence, as we can expect that these customs would attract the notice of Western ethnographers. For another example, when avoidance relationships as a type are discussed, or when parent-child and brother-sister relationships are examined, and there is no mention of father-daughter or brother-sister avoidance, these are coded absent. However, the codings for societal positions open to women are a little less certain: if women's positions are not mentioned, we cannot reasonably assume that they do not exist, because they may simply have escaped the ethnographer's notice. In this case, I coded absent only if there were statements to that effect or if there were extensive discussions of political and religious positions and women were not mentioned. I coded no information in doubtful cases.

When the coding was completed, I decided by inspection which of the variables to include in the tests, discarding only a few which were extremely limited in extent (such as the fascinating custom of groom capture, reported only for Garo and Minangkabau), and to some degree rearranging the others to make them suitable for machine testing. The code book, Appendix C, gives the final variables. Variables 1-44 were taken from the code sheets. Variables 45-54 were taken from the *Ethnographic Atlas* (Murdock 1967), with the exception of Variable 47 (see below).

DATA FROM THE *ETHNOGRAPHIC ATLAS*

Variable 45. Agriculture was coded Casual, Shifting, Horticulture, or Intensive (including Murdock's Irrigation Agriculture), according to placement in Column 28.

Variable 46. Intensity of animal use comes from Column 39, in which presence or absence of domesticated animals is indicated. Information on herding comes from Column

7, fourth digit. If this is 5, indicating 46-55 percent dependence on domesticated animals, or greater, the society is
considered to have a herding economy. The nonherding
societies that I coded present for intensive animal use are
Crow, Tlingit, and Tsimshian, which are known from the
literature to have derived a large, storable surplus of animal
foods from rich resources and sophisticated extraction
techniques.

Variable 47. Intensive trade is coded present according
to participation in a market economy. This is true if (a)
there is consistent production of goods specifically for exchange outside the network of socially-derived reciprocal
obligations, or (b) a majority of families are directly involved through at least one of their members in local or
long-distance exchange going beyond the social network.
This excludes such things as potlatches and kula rings.
African societies were sometimes difficult to code. For
example, I coded absent when the direct effects of trade
were limited to a small sector. Thus, Bemba was coded
absent even though the "Bemba state rose and flourished
on the basis of a localized monopoly of the trade in slaves
and ivory" (Stevenson 1968: 88), because this monopoly
was restricted to the political elite. Where there was evidence of trade meets or fairs held annually or oftener, I
coded present. For example, the Crow were coded present
for this trait, as they were well integrated into the cross-
continental horse trade at the time of their peak and held
trade meets with whites and with other Indians at which
large numbers of horses, furs, and trade goods exchanged
hands. (Although this variable was derived from primary
sources rather than from the *Ethnographic Atlas*, I put it in
this section to facilitate the reading of the code book.)

Variable 48. Intensity of craft specialization is derived
from Columns 42-60 in the *Ethnographic Atlas*, referring to
full-time specialization. If only one craft receives full-time
specialization, it is coded minimal. If two or more receive
specialization, the society is coded intensive for this trait.

Variable 49. Social stratification information is taken
from Columns 67, "Class Stratification," and 69, "Caste

Stratification." Stratification present but low is indicated by 67W, impermanent social division by wealth, and/or 69D, presence of one or more despised occupational groups. Medium stratification is indicated by 67D or 67E and/or 69E, presence of two major ranked groups. High stratification is indicated by 67C and/or 69C, complex stratification.

Variable 50. The information for the political integration scale is taken from Column 32, "Jurisdictional Hierarchy," second digit, which measures the number of jurisdictional levels transcending the local community. Murdock states: "The second digit incidentally provides a measure of political complexity, ranging from 0 for stateless societies, through 1 or 2 for petty and larger paramount chiefdoms or their equivalent, to 3 or 4 for large states" (Murdock 1967: 52). If we considered only the second digit, however, we would be ignoring the difference between a simple hunting band, such as the Tiwi, and a politically well-organized village polity, with rules for the transmission of authority, such as the Hopi. Murdock codes the Tiwi as 30 and the Hopi as 40. Therefore, among those societies which receive a 0 in Murdock's coding for the second digit, I distinguish between those with an initial number of 3 and 4. The former are coded for minimal integration, and the latter are coded for low integration. Societies with a second digit of 1 or 2 are coded for medium integration, and those with second digits of 3 or 4 are coded for high integration.

Variable 51. The information on spatial mobility comes from Column 30, "Settlement Pattern." Societies exhibiting settlement patterns coded B (nomadic), S (seminomadic), or T (semisedentary) were considered to have high mobility. Those coded H (separated hamlets) or W (compact but impermanent settlements) were considered to have medium mobility. Those coded V (compact permanent settlements) or X (complex settlements) were considered to have low mobility. For N (neighborhoods of dispersed family settlements), I referred to primary sources to get the mobility rating.

Variables 52-54. Information on residence pattern is

taken from Column 16, "Marital Residence." I divided avunculocal into two forms. Avunculocal residence combined with a preference for matrilateral cross-cousin marriage I considered to be wife-centered residence, whereas avunculocal residence without such preference I considered to be husband-centered. In the former case, it is not necessary that all or even a majority of actual marriages follow the preference: the point is that social rules accommodate such a preference. Therefore, if there is a congruence between wife-centered residence and other traits, we might expect to find it with this type of avunculocality.

In all cases I followed Murdock's coding unless I had clear evidence to the contrary. I list the corrections I made:

Darfur. While Murdock (1967) codes residence 0 (duolocal), both Beaton (1943: 12) and Felkin (1885: 234) indicate matrilocality.

Hopi. Murdock codes irrigation agriculture "present." Actually, this is true on such a small scale that it seems more appropriate to code "present" for horticulture.

Minangkabau. Murdock codes Jurisdictional Hierarchy (Column 32) as 40. Minangkabau was a kingdom until taken over by the Dutch and should have a coding of at least 41 (whether under precolonial or colonial conditions), which is what I have given it.

Siuai. Murdock codes the residential pattern vAu. I code it V, on the basis of the predominance of patrilocal arrangements (Oliver 1955: 234-40).

Talamanca. Murdock codes residence pattern as uNv. Stone (1962: 29) indicates patrilocality.

Tuareg. Murdock codes irrigation agriculture "present," by which he must be referring to date cultivation. My sources refer to exclusively herding peoples, so I coded agriculture "absent."

In addition, Gure was not coded by Murdock for these traits, so that coding I did myself.

Under ideal conditions, a completely explicit code book would be written and each of the societies would then be coded independently by two or more ethnographers who had done fieldwork there at about the same time. Thus would all coder error be eliminated, any error being source error; and the data would be comparable, as they would pertain to both the same place and the same time for each society. This ideal can rarely be met. The coding procedures I have delineated in this chapter are designed to treat the material that is available, scanty or ambiguous though it sometimes may be, as carefully as possible.

5

Testing

The nature of the data, which is nominal, limits the number and the sophistication of the statistical procedures that can be applied to it. The basic statistic I have used is the chi square. Where results are significant at the .05 level or greater, I have interpreted this as indicating that distribution is not random. There are several factors which must be taken into account here. First, the smaller the expected frequency in each cell of the contingency table, the less secure are the results. An arbitrary cut-off point for the applicability of the chi square at the expected frequency of less than five per cell is common.

Second, the smaller the total number of cases, the less likely one is to get statistically significant results (Blalock 1964: 227); so that with a sample as small as 66 cases, statistically significant results are likely to be theoretically significant as well.

Third, the chi square statistic is insensitive to the direction of relationship. I quote Blalock on this point:

> We can take advantage of predictions as to the direction simply by halving the significance level obtained. If chi square is large enough to yield significance at the .10 level without predicting direction, the result will be significant at the .05 level provided, of course, that the direction of the relationship was predicted beforehand [Blalock 1964: 218].

Therefore, where the direction has been predicted, the results are considerably more significant, statistically and theoretically, than the probability would indicate. In interpreting results, it is necessary to take all of these points into consideration.

As I have already indicated, the basic statistic in this study is the chi square. I have used Fisher's Exact Test for those tables for which the chi square test was not appropriate. In Chapter 7, I present the raw numbers arranged in tabular form, as well as raw chi square, probability, and contingency coefficient, so that the reader can check my interpretations.

Most of the statistical procedures were done by computer. The program I used is the Statistical Package for the Social Sciences.

6

Trustworthiness

There are two kinds of errors that the cross-cultural researcher must avoid. The first, and less important, is the random error, the result of inadvertently writing down the wrong number, misinterpreting a statistic, using a datum that is incorrect, etc. It is assumed that the scholar uses ordinary care in avoiding this type of error so far as is possible. One takes comfort in the knowledge that random error depresses correlations, so that those that do appear do so in spite of random error.

The second kind, the one that is likely to call into question his findings, is the systematic error. This type is dangerous because it can bias one or more of the findings, thus leading to false associations. Systematic error can arise at each of the procedural steps: selection of sources, coding, and interpretations. (For a detailed discussion of error and its control, see Naroll 1962.) In this chapter I shall examine each of these steps and outline the precautions taken to avoid systematic error.

ERROR AT THE SOURCE

In his book *Data Quality Control* (1962), Naroll goes into some detail to explain the need for procedures by which to check the trustworthiness of data. The rationale behind these procedures is that the kinds of data that can be consistently associated with some factor about the ethnographer—e.g. his length of stay, knowledge of the native language, nationality, etc.—might lead to spurious correlations which are artifacts of reportage rather than functional associations. As Naroll states:

> We wish to see whether correlations between traits being studied are artifacts of reporting conditions. To do this, we correlate each trait with each data quality control indicator: if one trait in a correlation proves related to the reporting conditions, we retain partial control; but if both traits prove so related, the correlation is out of control and partial analysis to allow for the influence of the reporting conditions is mandatory [Naroll 1962: 17].

Source trustworthiness was tested on two grounds, quantity and quality of data. Furthermore, for this type of study, which delves into the intimacies of sexual relations and family life, it seemed to me that the sex of the ethnographer might have considerable influence on the kind of data reported. One might expect, for example, that co-wife jealousy and menstrual restrictions would come more to the notice of the woman ethnographer than to the man. Therefore, I ran a control test on this variable also. To test for source bias, I took each of these three variables and tested all other variables against them.

Quantity of Data

I coded each society according to whether it was poorly reported (under 100 pages of ethnography available to me), adequately reported (100 to 250 pages), or well reported (over 250 pages, or with shorter but detailed reports on kinship and family life). Fourteen societies were poorly reported, 10 were adequately reported, and 42 were well reported. The highest proportion of poorly reported societies was from Africa, with 7 out of 20, or 35 percent. Next came South America, with 2 out of 7, or 28.6 percent. North America, with 2 out of 15, had 14.3 percent poorly reported. Asia and Oceania each had 12.5 percent poorly reported, with 1 out of 8 and 2 out of 16, respectively. To those who are interested in increasing our knowledge about matrilineal societies, this suggests that more work be done in Africa on known but poorly reported societies, and also in South America, to uncover unreported societies. The African material, particularly, is disappointing: while there is an abundance of work done in the region around Ashanti and in the "matrilineal belt," reports from other parts are spotty. It makes one wonder if the "matrilineal belt" is not an artifact of reportage.

I ran tests using quantity of data as the dependent variable against all other variables. The resulting chi square statistics reached the .05 level of significance in only two tables, quality of data and woman exchange. The first is to be expected, as ethnographers who stay a shorter time in the field are likely to write shorter reports (see below for a discussion on quality of data). As to woman exchange, I account for this by the small number of cases in which it was coded "present," 5 out of 60 cases for which there were data. For no other variable is there evidence that the quantity of data skewed the findings. As might be expected, the higher the quantity rating, the more the codings of "present" and "absent" and the fewer the codings of "no information."

Quality of Data

Each society was rated as to the trustworthiness of the source or sources. If the major ethnographer, or one of the others relied upon strongly in the coding, had spent at least one year in the society and spoke the native language, that society received a rating of high trustworthiness. If neither of these conditions was present, it received a low trustworthiness rating. If only one was present—i.e. if the ethnographer had been there at least one year but did not speak the language, or had been there under a year and did—the society received a rating of medium trustworthiness. If two or more persons went as a team and stayed six months or more, I considered this equal to one year. A rating of low trustworthiness does not discredit the data: some of our best accounts, indeed some of our only ones, are from "low trustworthiness" sources. We are dealing in probabilities, and it is probable that knowledge of the society improves with length of stay and knowledge of the native language (Naroll 1962: 87-90).

I was able to get trustworthiness information for all so-cieties but two: Santa Cruz and Longudu. I had neglected to ask William Davenport, who coded Santa Cruz, his length of stay; and for Longudu, there was no information given in the report. Of the remaining 64 societies, 22 had a rating of low trustworthiness, 7 a rating of medium trust-worthiness, and 35 a rating of high trustworthiness.

I took trustworthiness rating as the dependent variable and tabulated it with every other variable. The χ^2 tables that showed a distribution of 5 percent or less due to chance were those dealing with quantity of data (variable 55), husband defers to wife's brother (variable 7), bride-wealth (variable 12), marriage disruption in another form (variable 15), co-wife jealousy (variable 22), and severity of sibling incest sanctions (variable 41).

The first has already been discussed above. The table for variable 7 may be skewed by the high rating of "absent" for high trustworthiness societies: 15 out of 20, out of a total of 29 cases for which there is evidence. For three variables there is a high rating of absent on low trustworthi-ness societies, variables 12, 15, and 22. Out of a total of 63 societies for which there is evidence, bridewealth is re-ported absent in 14 of the low trustworthiness societies. Out of a total of 34 societies, marriage disruption in an-other form is reported absent in 10 out of 11 low trust-worthiness societies. Out of 41 societies, co-wife jealousy is reported absent in 9 of the 11 low trustworthiness cases. It may be that length of stay and/or knowledge of the lan-guage improves the ethnographer's chance of finding these traits present.

As for variable 41, there may be a tendency for long-staying or native language-speaking ethnographers to rate sibling incest sanctions as severe. Out of the 25 societies for which severe sanctions were coded "present," 17 were high trustworthiness. The only cases of sibling incest permitted, Guanche and Ambo, were low trustworthiness societies.

Sex of Major Researcher

Fifty-two of the major ethnographers were men, and 14 were women. I took sex as the dependent variable and tabulated all other variables against it. The results were surprising—sex of reporter appears to make very little difference in the kind or amount of data reported. Only two of the tables were significant at the .05 level or less, ascribed position shared with men (variable 30) and polyandry (variable 23). For the former, out of the 46 cases for which there was information, 36 were reported by men (25 absent, 11 present), and 10 were reported by women (3 absent, 7 present). I do not consider this important, as none of the other variables relating to women's position in society show statistically significant distribution.

The findings on polyandry, however, are a little more difficult to explain away. Out of 59 societies for which there was evidence, polyandry was reported present in 11, an unexpectedly high number. Of these 11, 5 were reported by men (as against 42 absent) and 6 by women (as against 6 absent). We can ask ourselves whether women tend to do fieldwork in polyandrous societies, whether they have a greater tendency to discover it, and/or whether they have a greater tendency to report it. One might imagine it highly gratifying to the woman ethnographer to explode the myth that women are "by nature" monogamous.

ERROR IN CODING

The best precaution against error in coding is the clearly written coding manual. Even this does not guard against two sources of untrustworthiness, source disagreement and coder disagreement over material open to more than one interpretation.

Source Disagreement

I had devised no rule about handling source disagreement when I began this study, nor do I think any single rule would cover the kinds of ethnographic discrepancies I found. One could devise a single rule, such as selecting for the ethnographer that stayed the longest or wrote the most pages; but here I prefer to rely upon the judgment of the trained cross-cultural researcher to select the best information. In any case in which discrepancy for a variable exceeds 10 percent of the reported cases, I would suggest the application of a single rule, as a precaution against the researcher consistently selecting for the choice that favors his hypothesis.

In this study, I selected for long versus short field time, knowledge of native language versus no knowledge, direct versus peripheral investigation of the subject, and anthropological training versus none, as increasing reliability. For the reader's elucidation, I report the disagreements and my reasons for choosing one report over another.

Creek: bridewealth. Speck (1907: 117) claims consent of the girl and her family only, while Swanton (1924-25: 369) mentions bridewealth. I chose the latter, because Swanton spent a total of a year doing fieldwork among the Creek, whereas Speck's observations were incidental to a study of the Yuchi.

Dieri: polyandry. Howitt, the major source, claims polyandry (Howitt 1890: 53). However, Elkin (1938: 76) discusses this question in some detail. He convinces me that the *pirauru* institution is not true marriage but privileged sexual relations.

Garo: husband's authority over wife and children. Nakane claims that the husband is the authority (Nakane 1967: 75), while Burling claims that it is the wife's brother (Burling 1963: 81-82, 168, 258). I take Burling's word on this, as he was in the field for two years while Nakane was among the Garo for less than five months. Furthermore, what Nakane gives as signs of authority appears to me to be deference behavior, which is not the same thing.

Iroquois: positions open to women. It came as something of a surprise to read in Morgan (1881: 122) that "this influence of the women did not reach outward to the affairs of the gens, phratry, or tribe, but seem to have commenced and ended with the household." Other authors indicate that women indeed did have positions of importance outside the home, and the quantity of evidence forces me to discount Morgan's statement on this point.

Palau: household authority. An ambiguous statement by Force leads me to infer that the husband has household authority. He states: "The male head of a household was considered the leader of the household, but his wife shared leadership honors with him" (Force 1960: 54). Barnett, on the other hand, speaks of a man as leader (*merrederer*) of his sister (Barnett 1949: 26) and of a woman's allegiance as being "naturally, as the Palauans see it, to her brothers and her mother's brother and not to her husband" (Barnett 1949: 62). I coded "brother authority" on the basis of Barnett's statements, in spite of the fact that Force was on Palau sixteen months whereas Barnett was there only nine (both spoke the language). The reason is that Barnett investigated family and kinship closely, while Force's discussion of family life was incidental to his study of traditional and contemporary social leadership.

Pawnee: substantial versus token bridewealth. Weltfish, the major source, mentions "a substantial gift of horses" (Weltfish 1965: 17). However, this is qualified by Grinnell (1891: 279), who indicates that most of these were reciprocated in the form of counter gifts after the wedding.

Coder Disagreement

As I have already mentioned, 16 of the 66 societies were coded by me alone and 48 with a cocoder (plus two by the ethnographers). I am responsible for the final coding choice in each case, although the final choice is not always my initial choice: in roughly 11 percent of the final choices I selected the cocoder's initial choice over my own.

Coder disagreement occurred when one coder coded "present" and the other "absent" for a trait. (I did not consider "no information" to be a disagreement with "present" or "absent.") As I had instructed the coders to be conservative, their codings showed a higher proportion of "no information" than did mine. On only two questions was there 20 percent or greater disagreement: I-D, Control Over Property, for which disagreement occurred in 12 cases, or 24 percent; and I-C4:1, Husband Agression, with 10 cases of disagreement, or 20 percent. There was disagreement in 8 cases of I-A, Authority Pattern, and in 8 cases of II-A3:5, Women Perform Publicly. For every other trait, there were 5 or fewer disagreements. The 8 societies for which there was disagreement on the most critical coding, Authority Pattern, are Bemba, Creek, Kurtatchi, Lesu, Ndembu, Palau, Ponape, and Suku.

ERROR IN INTERPRETATION

Replicability

Interpretation is based in the first place upon the data. So that the reader can check the interpretations against the data, I have given sources and page references for each of the decisions coded. These are recorded in Appendix B.

World Area

A major interpretation error is the making of general statements about the nature of an association between traits when this is in fact found only in one part of the world or when the great majority of associations are localized. To prevent this error from invalidating my results, I took world area as an independent variable and tested all variables against it. The breakdown of societies by world area is as follows: Africa—20, 30.3 percent; Asia—8, 12.1 percent; Oceania—16, 24.2 percent; South America—7, 10.6 percent; North America—15, 22.7 percent.

There is some clustering of "present" and "absent" according to world area, which I shall survey here.

Domestic Authority Pattern (variable 4): the distribution is skewed toward high Husband Dominant for Africa and high Neither Dominant for North America.

Divorce (variable 13): Africa and Oceania show a high incidence of "Wife Leaves," while Asia and North America show a high incidence of "Husband Leaves."

Husband Aggression (variable 16): Africa and Oceania show a high incidence of this trait.

Brother Aggression (variable 17): this trait is most strongly represented in Asia.

Control of Property (variable 19): exclusive male control (husband and/or brother) is strong in Africa and Oceania, while total or shared female control is strong in Asia and North America.

Sororal Polygyny (variable 21): Africa shows a strong preference against this trait, while North and South America show a strong preference for it.

Menstrual Restrictions (variable 33): North America has the highest incidence of reported restrictions and the highest incidence of menstrual seclusion.

Menstrual Restrictions Protect Others (variable 35): out of five cases reported absent, three are from Oceania. (This I consider an insignificant finding, as the numbers involved are so small.)

Blood Endangers Ritual Objects (variable 36) and Blood Endangers the Food Supply (variable 37): in both cases most of the data come from North America, and in each case "present" greatly outweighs "absent."

Residence (variables 52-53): Africa and Oceania show a high incidence of Husband-Centered Residence, while Asia and North America show a high incidence of Wife-Centered Residence.

The purpose of presenting these findings is to alert the reader to the possibility of spurious associations; i.e. two traits may appear to be functionally related because they are both represented in the same societies to a statistically significant degree, when in fact they have diffused independently within the same area. This problem will be discussed more fully in the next section of this chapter. Therefore, if we find a positive correlation between Husband-Centered Residence and Husband Aggression, for example, we cannot rule out the possibility of diffusional effects. On the other hand, if we find an association between traits that are significantly associated with different world areas, such as Husband-Centered Residence and Menstrual Restrictions, or between one trait associated with a world area and another not so associated, we can assume that our correlation is not explained by localized diffusion.

Independent Diffusion

In Chapter 3 we discussed Galton's problem and the importance of selecting culturally independent cases for the sample, and in the preceding section of this chapter we examined the danger of assuming a correlation to be general when it is in fact limited to a localized area. In this section, we shall discuss another error in interpretation, the assumption that a correlation is general when the two traits involved can have codiffused independently.

If we can show that the trait associations we are concerned with occur independently of geographic contiguity, then they cannot be said to be solely the result of coincidental codiffusion. To discover whether or not this is the case, Naroll has devised a series of testing methods using contiguity as a measure of diffusion (for a summary, see Naroll 1965). One of these is the Linked Pair method. This is a series of five tests. Two of them test for diffusion on world-wide alignments along north-south and east-west axes. Two others do the same within each continent. The fifth employs a sample of societies plotted along arcs which cross-cut longitudinal and latitudinal lines.

For this study, I use the first two tests. I have already tested for intracontinental diffusion by using world area as the dependent variable in the series of chi square tests (see above). The fifth would be unsuitable for this particular study, which requires a sample of matrilineal societies only.

The tests have been programed for the computer. For the present study, they were conducted at the State University of New York, Buffalo, Computing Center, through the gracious cooperation of Raoul Naroll. For all these tests, the variables were dichotomized, and the linked pair test for cultural diffusion was performed. Association was measured by the phi coefficient, and the statistical significance of the resultant association was computed by Fisher's Exact

Test. The result of these tests approached significance for only five variables as follows:

TABLE 1: 6 Linked Pair Test for Cultural Diffusion

| Variables | East-West | | North-South | |
	Phi	Exact Probability	Phi	Exact Probability
Divorce—Wife Leaves	.25	.04	.44	.0005
Divorce—Husband Leaves	.16	.16	.35	.005
Sibling Incest Taboos Broadly Extended	.39	.018	−.07	.99
Craft Specialization	.26	.034	.30	.019
Bride Capture	.17	.21	.43	.006

Neither the authority patterns nor any of the variables discussed in detail show any indication of significant diffusion. I therefore consider diffusion not to be a factor leading to the statistically significant results of this study.

This chapter has been concerned with error and the steps taken to control for it. We have discussed errors at the source and the data quality control procedures, of the type devised by Raoul Naroll, that have been used for dealing with such errors. Possible coding errors, whether due to source disagreement or coder disagreement, have been examined. Neither of these kinds of disagreement exists to such a degree as to cast reasonable doubt on the findings. As for errors of interpretation, the major difficulty here is in interpreting associations as functional when in fact they could be coincidental results of diffusion. Two kinds of tests were conducted—a test for localized diffusion within a world area and tests for diffusion along longitudinal and latitudinal axes—and neither of these indicated that any of the major hypotheses of this study were in danger of misinterpretation due to spurious association. In addition, the section on "Replicability" points out to the reader how the coding decisions can be checked if any are held in doubt.

While these kinds of checking procedures may seem tedious and drawn-out, they are necessary to validate the statistical associations, or findings. Single-case or concomitant variation studies can still contribute much in the way of insight and stimulus, even if one argues with the findings—I hold up as an example Robert Redfield's *Tepoztlan* (1930) and Oscar Lewis's restudy, *Life in a Mexican Village* (1951), which disputed Redfield's findings. The cross-cultural study, however, must stand or fall on the correctness of its findings. One may agree or disagree with the conclusions, but errors in sampling, coding, and interpretation will invalidate the study, no matter how elegantly it may have been conceived or presented.

The next chapter gives the findings.

7

The Findings

The statistical operations, and the directions they take, given below confirm the hypothesis that underlies this study: that the theoretical division of matrilineal domestic organization into authority types conforms to the real world. These types not only exist but also have attached to them groups of variables constituting authority type syndromes. These variables are not necessarily mutually exclusive from type to type; i.e. there are variables which characterize both Husband Authority and Brother Authority but not Type III, etc. What we find are various combinations of features reflecting female subordination or lack of it, affiliation of the woman to one or the other of the significant same-generation male kin, and varying degrees of affiliation of minor children to the descent or the domestic group authorities. Rarely is a variable found associated with only a single authority type. This should not be surprising, as the domestic group is a complex institution which is not only a system within itself but also part of the entire social and cultural system. We can create boundaries, but these must be understood to be artificial, or, better perhaps, permeable; for the rules and relationships that govern the domestic group must coordinate with the rules and relationships that govern sociocultural behavior in toto.

In this chapter I present the findings. I include within the body of the chapter those tables which yield significant or near-significant results. A fuller discussion is reserved for subsequent chapters. Where I indicate C, the contingency coefficient, it is uncorrected: corrections for the two-by-two tables would raise the results. Nonsignificant tables appear in an appendix at the end of the chapter. (Compare with Appendix C, Code Book.)

I have collapsed the five domestic authority types into three: Husband Dominant, Neither Dominant, and Brother Dominant. This is because there are too few societies at either end of the gradient to allow for statistical manipulations. In all instances, where an hypothesis was confirmed by statistical tests, the cases at the extreme ends, Types I and V, were in conformity with the cases in the lesser dominance categories, Types II and IV respectively.

The breakdown is as follows: Type I, strong husband authority—7; Type II, lesser husband authority—22; Type III—neither husband nor brother authority—14; Type IV, lesser brother authority—18; Type V, strong brother authority—3. When collapsed, this gives the figures of 29 for Husband Dominant, 14 for Neither Dominant, and 21 for Brother Dominant. There is a total of 64 cases, as there are two societies, Locono and Longudu, for which I could extract no information whatsoever on domestic authority.

What follows are the results of the tests using Variable 4, Domestic Authority Type, as the dependent variable in relation to all other variables, excluding the quality control variables, which have already been examined. Unless otherwise indicated, my findings refer to the three dominance types. In some cases, when the tripartite division did not yield significant results, I collapsed data and tested one type in relation to the other two for presence or absence of that trait. In those cases in which there appears by inspec-

TABLE 1: 7.   Variable 5: Wife Defers to Husband
(Number of cases: 51)

	Absent	Present
Husband Dominant	4	19
Neither Dominant	11	1
Brother Dominant	5	11

$\chi^2 = 18.9$ $p < .01$ C=.52

tion to be a clear tendency, but for which (because of test restrictions) neither the chi square nor Fisher's Exact Test can be used, I have let the tables stand without tests for significance.

To determine which authority types were responsible for this distribution, I tested Husband Dominant alone against the other two combined, in other words Husband Dominant versus non-Husband Dominant. This relationship is significant: $p < .01$. It is apparent, as one would expect, that wife-to-husband deference is highly characteristic of Husband Dominant societies. However, this form of deference may also be part of a general female-to-male deference pattern; so I tested Brother Dominant versus Neither Dominant, which yielded chi square at the $< .01$ significance level. This indicates that this deference pattern characterizes both Husband Dominant and Brother Dominant societies, in contrast to its absence in Neither Dominant societies.

TABLE 2: 7.   Variable 6: Sister Defers to Brother
(Number of cases: 39)

	Absent	Present
Husband Dominant	11	4
Neither Dominant	11	0
Brother Dominant	1	12

$\chi^2 = 23.1$ $p < .001$ C=.60

This tells us that sister-to-brother deference is highly characteristic of Brother Dominant societies. (In the four Husband Dominant societies for which it was reported present—Coniagui, Darfur, Ndembu, and Santa Cruz—wife-to-husband deference was also present; so in these instances sister deference can be considered part of a generalized female deference.)

Variable 7: Husband Defers to Wife's Brother (Number of cases: 30)

The first test yielded nonsignificant results. However, in the testing of Brother Dominant versus non-Brother Dominant, the results were p <.10, suggesting that deference to wife's brother may be characteristic of Brother Dominant societies. If bride givers are superior to bride takers, as this distribution suggests, they appear to be so primarily in Brother Dominant societies.

Variable 9: Bride Capture (Number of cases: 63)
All seven societies for which this trait is coded "present" are in the Husband Dominant category. It is therefore an indicator of husband authority rather than an associated variable. In the five-type breakdown, 4 out of the 7 cases of Type I have this feature, as compared with 3 out of the 22 Type II societies. It is therefore most closely associated with strong husband authority.

There were not enough cases of groom capture to merit inclusion in the test—only two, the Minangkabau and Garo. The former is symbolic capture, as part of the wedding ceremony, but the latter is true capture, with the groom consenting to remain, if at all, only after several attempts to escape and abject pleading on the part of his bride. These are both Brother Dominant societies, and therefore groom capture is not the obverse of bride capture; i.e. it does not reflect the authority of the wife over the husband, which would be plausible if it were found in Neither Dominant societies. Note that Garo wives defer to their husbands, another indication that groom capture does not indicate matriarchy. This is yet another example illustrating that extreme caution must be applied when assuming that similar traits have similar meanings.

It appears that the Husband Dominant distribution is having the strongest effect; so I performed two tests of Husband Dominant against non-Husband Dominant. The

TABLE 3:7. Variable 10: Bridewealth
(Number of cases: 63)

	Absent	Substantial	Token
Husband Dominant	10	13	6
Neither Dominant	8	1	5
Brother Dominant	12	4	4

first, in which I tested for presence or absence of bride-wealth, yielded p < .05. The second, in which I combined "absent" and "token" and tested this against "substantial," resulted in p < .01. The second test supports my hypothesis that substantial bridewealth differs from token bridewealth. Both tests together show that bridewealth is more characteristic of Husband Dominant societies than the other two types. I believe we are justified in concluding that bride-wealth, or at least substantial bridewealth, buys rights over the woman.

Although the test for Variable 11, Bride Service, did not yield significant results, a test combining bride service with bridewealth (with societies having both being counted only once each) was significant at the > .02 level, testing Husband Dominant against non-Husband Dominant. Thus, bride service can also be considered a form of payment for the woman.

Variable 12: Woman Exchange (Number of cases: 60)
All five cases reported "present" are in the Husband Dominant category, 3 in Type I and 2 in Type II. Woman exchange is therefore an indicator of husband authority, and strong authority at that. Taken in connection with the two preceding variables, this supports my hypothesis that woman exchange is an extreme form of bridewealth, or payment for rights over the woman.

The distribution indicates a strong association between wife leaving and Husband Dominant, on the one hand, and husband leaving and both Neither Dominant and Brother Dominant, on the other. The surprise in these findings is

TABLE 4: 7.   Variable 13: Divorce
(Number of cases: 64; cases tested: 57)

	Absent*	Wife Leaves	Husband Leaves	Other*
Husband Dominant	1	21	6	1
Neither Dominant	1	3	8	2
Brother Dominant	0	7	12	2

χ^2=11.1776   p < .01   C=.40

*not tested

TABLE 5:7. Variable 14: Wife's Brother Disrupts Marriage
(Number of cases: 43)

	Absent	*Present*
Husband Dominant	15	4
Neither Dominant	8	0
Brother Dominant	2	14

$\chi^2 = 22.8$ $p < .001$ C=.59

that in Neither Dominant domestic groups the balance is so strongly weighted in favor of the wife, with the husband leaving in 72.7 percent of the cases.

This finding is important in light of the popular assumption in anthropology that women in matrilineal societies "belong" to their descent groups more than they do in other, particularly patrilineal, societies. There is no indication here that there is a generalized right in matrilineal societies for the wife's lineal kin to invade the privacy of her domestic group, unless that group is itself under the authority of her male kin.

TABLE 6:7. Variable 16: Husband Aggression
(Number of cases: 45)

	Absent	*Present*
Husband Dominant	3	21
Neither Dominant	6	3
Brother Dominant	2	10

Clearly, the similarity here is between Husband Dominant and Brother Dominant societies, of which 88 percent and 83.3 percent, respectively, allow husband aggression as I have defined it. They are dissimilar to Neither Dominant societies, of which 66.6 percent do not allow it.

TABLE 7:7. Variable 17: Brother Aggression
(Number of cases: 26)

	Absent	*Present*
Husband Dominant	10	1
Neither Dominant	6	0
Brother Dominant	0	9

It requires no statistical testing to show that brother aggression is strongly associated positively with Brother Dominant societies and negatively with the other two types. This is to be expected.

TABLE 8: 7. Variable 18: Control of Children
(Number of cases: 60)

(This excludes the three cases of absence of male control over children: 1 Husband Dominant and 2 Neither Dominant)

	Father	Mother's Brother	Shared
Husband Dominant	19	2	7
Neither Dominant	7	4	1
Brother Dominant	2	16	2

$\chi^2 = 27.9$ $p < .001$ C=.56

This highly significant finding is in the predicted direction for husband and brother authority. An interesting feature is the degree to which control over minor children is shared by the father and mother's brother in Husband Dominant societies, 25 percent of all cases. This reminds us that authority over the wife is not tautologically associated with control over her children, and that the matrilineal pull is felt even in some groups in which the husband is the domestic authority. However, this is true only for Type II

TABLE 9: 7. Variable 19: Control Over Property
(Number of cases: 58)

	1	2	3	4	5	6	7
Husband Dominant	1	16	6	1	0	0	0
Neither Dominant	0	0	10	3	1	0	0
Brother Dominant	0	0	6	2	1	8	3

(1—absent; 2—husband control; 3—husband and wife share control; 4—woman control; 5—brother and sister share control; 6—brother control; 7—husband and brother share control.)

See Table 1: 8, p. 86

societies: the 7 Type I societies are exclusively "father control."

There is a clear association between husband control and Husband Dominant societies, and brother control and Brother Dominant societies. This distribution will be explored more fully (see Table 1: 8, p. 86).

The tendency among Neither Dominant societies is toward female participation in control of domestic group property. Of the 14 Neither Dominant cases, 3 have total female control, 11 have control shared by the woman with husband or brother, and none have all male control. In contrast, for the 44 Husband Dominant and Brother Dominant cases, 3 have total female control, 13 have shared male-female control, and 27 have all male control. Of the total sample, the largest single category is control shared by husband and wife: 37.9 percent. The next largest category is total husband control: 27.6 percent.

These findings are suggestive of the relatively strong voice of women concerning domestic group property, outside the Husband Dominant category. However, the sample includes 33 cases, or 46.6 percent, in which there is total male control. I am unable at present to say how this would compare with a sample of nonmatrilineal societies.

TABLE 10: 7. Variable 20: Polygyny
(Number of cases: 64)

	Absent	Limited	General
Husband Dominant	2	16	11
Neither Dominant	5	7	2
Brother Dominant	1	15	5

The skewing effect here seems to be the higher proportion of absence of polygyny in Neither Dominant societies, 35.7 percent, as compared with Husband Dominant societies (6.9 percent) and Brother Dominant societies (4.8 percent).

Here it appears to be the absence of polygyny, and the absence of preference against the sororal form, in Neither

TABLE 11: 7.   Variable 21: Sororal Polygyny
(Number of cases: 46)

	Absent	No Preference	Preference for	Preference against
Husband Dominant	2	6	7	5
Neither Dominant	5	1	3	0
Brother Dominant	0	3	5	9

Dominant societies that are important. In other words, none of the Neither Dominant societies for which we have data have a rule that two or more sisters cannot marry the same man. This means that there is no *necessary* fragmenting of the domestic group into separate co-wife units when the husband takes secondary wives, as there is where the preference is against sororal polygyny. The numbers are too small to generalize, however.

TABLE 12: 7.   Variable 22: Co-Wife Jealousy
(Number of cases: 42)

	Absent	Present
Husband Dominant	6	14
Neither Dominant	7	3
Brother Dominant	8	4

$\chi^2 = 6.13$ $p < .05$ C=.36

It is obviously the Husband Dominant cells that are exerting the pull: testing Husband Dominant against non-Husband Dominant yields results significant at the $> .01$ level. This highly interesting finding about the nature of domestic group sentiments will be discussed in a subsequent chapter.

Variable 23: Polyandry (see Table 27: 7)
While the findings are not significant at the .05 level, it is interesting to note that at least 16.7 percent of the total sample of 66 societies allows polyandry, or 18.6 percent of those societies for which we have data. It is unlikely that this high a percentage would be duplicated using a nonmatrilineal sample. To what degree polyandry is char-

TABLE 13: 7.   Variable 26: Wife's Adultery Punished
(Number of cases: 49)

	Absent	Husband Punishes	Brother Punishes
Husband Dominant	2	20	2
Neither Dominant	8	4	0
Brother Dominant	2	7	4

acteristic of matrilineal societies cannot be answered at this time.

There seem to be two possible interpretations for this distribution: husband and brother have differing punitive roles in Husband Dominant and Brother Dominant societies; and wife's adultery is more likely to be punished in male dominant than in Neither Dominant societies. I therefore conducted two tests. In the first, I tested Husband Dominant in relation to Brother Dominant for "husband punishes" versus "brother punishes." This yielded results significant at the $< .05$ level. In the second, I tested Neither Dominant in relation to non-Neither Dominant for "absence of punishment" versus "presence of punishment," with results significant at the $< .001$ level. Husband Dominant and Brother Dominant are more alike than either is like Neither Dominant in punishing wife's adultery, but there is a greater tendency for the brother to punish the wife in Brother Dominant than in Husband Dominant societies. It is interesting to note that in both cases, the majority of societies leave punishment of the wife to the husband, again showing the limitations to the interference of the woman's kin with her domestic group even in matrilineal societies.

TABLE 14: 7.   Variable 28: Ascribed Positions Exclusive to Women
(Number of cases: 40)

	Absent	Present
Husband Dominant	13	4
Neither Dominant	3	6
Brother Dominant	10	4

$\chi^2 = 5.20$ $p < .07$ C=.34

Variable 27: Husband Disposes of Wife's Sexuality (Number of cases: 33)

All seven of the cases reported "present" are in the Husband Dominant category.

This is close to the .05 level of significance. Testing Neither Dominant against non-Neither Dominant by Fisher's Exact Test yielded p = .028. There are more ascribed female status positions in Neither Dominant societies than in either of the male dominant ones.

TABLE 15:7. Variable 39: Preferential Marriage
(Number of cases: 61)

	1	3	4	5
Husband Dominant	13	9	3	1
Neither Dominant	13	1	0	0
Brother Dominant	9	5	7	0

(1—absent; 3—preference for matrilateral cross-cousin marriage; 4—preference for patrilateral cross-cousin marriage; 5—Ego marries woman related through his mother.)

Two features emerge from this distribution. First, there is an absence of preferential cross-cousin marriage in Neither Dominant societies, which was predicted. Second, there is a difference of preference between Husband Dominant and Brother Dominant societies. I tested Husband Dominant in relation to non-Husband Dominant for "preference for matrilateral cross-cousin marriage" versus "no preference for this form." The result was p < .10. This is nonsignificant as it stands, but suggestive of a tendency for Husband Dominant societies to prefer matrilateral cross-cousin marriage. (If we recall Blalock's advice [1964] that prediction doubles significance, then this finding is significant at the > .05 level—see p. 44.) Then I tested Brother Dominant in relation to non-Brother Dominant for "preference for patrilateral cross-cousin marriage" versus "no preference for this form." The result, using Fisher's Exact Test, was p=.014. Testing Husband Dominant against Brother Dominant for preference for the patrilateral form versus preference for the matrilateral form yielded p=.008, by

Fisher's Exact Test. This indicates a tendency which is lifted into significance by the fact of previous prediction.

Using Fisher's Exact Test, Husband Dominant was tested against Brother Dominant for Sibling Worse versus Father-Daughter Worse, with p=.005.

TABLE 16: 7.   Variable 40: Direction of Incest Taboo
(Number of cases: 27)

	Sibling Worse	Equal	Father-Daughter Worse
Husband Dominant	3	2	6
Neither Dominant	2	2	0
Brother Dominant	12	0	0

The sample is very small. However, with such highly significant test results, I feel safe in considering my hypothesis concerning the direction of the incest taboo confirmed; i.e. sibling incest tends to be worse in Brother Dominant societies, father-daughter incest tends to be worse in Husband Dominant societies, and no clear pattern is observed in Neither Dominant societies. The pull of matrilineality is indicated by the high proportion of societies which consider sibling incest worse, 63 percent. In spite of the smallness of the sample, I consider this to be one of the most important findings of the study.

Variable 42: Nonextension of Incest Taboo (Number of cases: 44)

The nine-cell table yielded no significant results. However, the figures suggested that there was a significant difference between Husband Dominant and the other two types. I collapsed "present: sexual relations allowed" and

TABLE 17: 7.   Nonextension of the Incest Taboo

	Absent	Present
Husband Dominant	13	8
Other	20	3

χ^2=3.67   p <.05   C=.28

"present: marriage allowed" into one category, "present." I
tested this against "absent" for Husband Dominant versus
non-Husband Dominant:

This test indicates that in the extension of the incest
taboos to classificatory siblings, Neither Dominant and
Brother Dominant societies are more alike than either is
like Husband Dominant. It also indicates, more important-
ly, that the pull is away from extension in Husband Dominant societies and toward it in the other two. In other
words, Husband Dominant societies are less likely to restrict marriage and sexual relations with classificatory
siblings than are Neither Dominant or Brother Dominant
societies. I believe that we can infer from this that there
tends to be less concern with sibling incest in Husband
Dominant societies than in the other two types. This
strengthens the findings of Variable 40, Direction of the
Incest Taboo, and gives me even greater confidence in
them.

Variable 48: Intensity of Craft Specialization (Number
of cases: 64)

The nine-cell table was tested, with no significant results.
However, testing Neither Dominant versus non-Neither
Dominant for presence or absence of specialization did
yield significant results:

TABLE 18: 7.   Intensity of Craft Specialization

	Absent	*Present*
Neither Dominant	13	1
Other	29	21

$\chi^2 = 5.89$ $p < .05$ C=.29

Since craft specialization is a measure of productivity,
albeit a weak one, I suggest that male dominance tends to
be found in the more productive societies.

Variable 49: Social Stratification (Number of cases: 64)

The results of the original test were nonsignificant. However, when Brother Dominant was tested in relation to non-
Brother Dominant for "absent and low stratification"

TABLE 19: 7. Social Stratification

	Absent-low	Medium-high
Brother Dominant	10	11
Other	32	11

$\chi^2 = 4.49$ $p < .05$ $C = .26$

versus "medium and high stratification," the results were significant:

This indicates that Husband Dominant and Neither Dominant societies tend to fall at the lower end of the social stratification gradient.

Variable 50: Political Integration (Number of cases: 64)

The first test yielded nonsignificant results. However, in the model, the Brother Dominant societies were clearly the more complex politically (with the exception of the Tuareg). I therefore retested, with significant results. I opposed Brother Dominant to non-Brother Dominant, and collapsed minimal and low integration into one column, and medium and high integration into another:

TABLE 20: 7. Political Integration

	Minimal-low	Medium-high
Brother Dominant	7	14
Other	27	16

$\chi^2 = 5.06$ $p < .05$ $C = .27$

This indicates that Brother Dominant societies tend toward medium-high political integration, while Husband Dominant and Neither Dominant societies tend toward minimal-low.

TABLE 21: 7. Variable 52: Wife-Centered Residence
(Number of cases: 64)

	1	2	3	4
Husband Dominant	21	1	4	4
Neither Dominant	4	0	10	0
Brother Dominant	11	0	8	2

(1—absent; 2—uxorilocal; 3—matrilocal; 4— avunculocal with preference for matrilateral cross-cousin marriage.)

The columns were collapsed into Absent (1) and Present (2, 3, 4) and tested by the chi square test. The results were $p < .05$, C=.30. The pull here appears to be between absence of this trait among Husband Dominant societies and presence of matrilocality among Neither Dominant ones.

TABLE 22:7.   Variable 53: Husband-Centered Residence
(Number of cases: 64)

	1	2	3	4
Husband Dominant	10	14	0	5
Neither Dominant	11	2	1	0
Brother Dominant	14	1	0	6

(1—absent; 2—virilocality; 3—patrilocality; 4—avunculocality without preference for matrilateral cross-cousin marriage.)

The columns were collapsed into Absent (1) and Present (2, 3, 4) and tested by the chi square test. The results were $p < .05$, C=.35. The pull here is between the high "present" for virilocal marriage among Husband Dominant societies and the high "Absent" for husband-centered residence among the other two types.

In this chapter I have presented the findings. I have attempted to present them in as straightforward a manner as possible, leaving the interpretations for the chapters to come. In order to conduct the statistical operations, I have had to collapse from five into three categories. This increases the generality of the findings.

The total number of probability and inspection tests conducted was 76. Of these, 33 yielded significant results, including those presented in Chapter 11. This is not likely to have resulted from chance.

The discussion so far has been concerned with presenting the hypotheses, the procedures used to test them (and the steps taken to protect against error in these procedures), and the results of the statistical tests. In the discussions that follow I interpret these findings.

Appendix to Chapter 7

TABLE 23: 7.   Variable 7: Husband Defers to Wife's Brother
(Number of cases: 30)

	Absent	Present
Husband Dominant	12	2
Neither Dominant	4	1
Brother Dominant	6	5

TABLE 24: 7.   Variable 8: Brother Defers to Sister's Husband
(Number of cases: 31)

	Absent	Present
Husband Dominant	12	2
Neither Dominant	6	0
Brother Dominant	9	2

TABLE 25: 7.   Variable 11: Bride Service
(Number of cases: 62)

	Absent	Substantial	Token
Husband Dominant	22	4	2
Neither Dominant	11	2	1
Brother Dominant	20	0	0

TABLE 26: 7.   Variable 15: Other Disruption of Marriage
(Number of cases: 35)

	Absent	Present
Husband Dominant	10	7
Neither Dominant	5	2
Brother Dominant	8	3

TABLE 27:7.   Variable 23: Polyandry
                   (Number of cases: 59)

	Absent	Present
Husband Dominant	24	3
Neither Dominant	9	5
Brother Dominant	15	3

TABLE 28:7.   Variable 24: Adultery Allowed for Husband
                   (Number of cases: 49)

	Absent	Present
Husband Dominant	7	15
Neither Dominant	5	7
Brother Dominant	8	7

TABLE 29:7.   Variable 25: Adultery Allowed for Wife
                   (Number of cases: 55)

	Absent	Present
Husband Dominant	19	7
Neither Dominant	6	6
Brother Dominant	13	4

TABLE 30:7.   Variable 29: Achieved Positions Exclusive to Women
                   (Number of cases: 39)

	Absent	Present
Husband Dominant	12	5
Neither Dominant	5	2
Brother Dominant	13	2

TABLE 31:7.   Variable 30: Ascribed Position Shared with Men
                   (Number of cases: 46)

	Absent	Present
Husband Dominant	13	9
Neither Dominant	4	5
Brother Dominant	11	4

TABLE 32: 7.   Variable 31: Achieved Positions Shared with Men
(Number of cases: 42)

	Absent	Present
Husband Dominant	9	11
Neither Dominant	4	4
Brother Dominant	8	6

TABLE 33: 7.   Variable 32: Women Perform Publicly
(Number of cases: 29)

	Absent	Present
Husband Dominant	4	6
Neither Dominant	2	7
Brother Dominant	4	6

TABLE 34: 7.   Variable 33: Severity of Menstrual Restrictions
(Number of cases: 45)

	1	2	3	4	5
Husband Dominant	0	5	5	4	5
Neither Dominant	1	6	1	3	1
Brother Dominant	0	7	2	2	3

(1—absent; 2—seclusion; 3—cooking taboo; 4—other restrictions; 5—sex taboo)

TABLE 35: 7.   Variable 34: Menstrual Restrictions Protect Women
(Number of cases: 30)

	Absent	Present
Husband Dominant	8	6
Neither Dominant	3	5
Brother Dominant	7	1

TABLE 36: 7.   Variable 35: Restrictions Protect Others
(Number of cases: 31)

	Absent	Present
Husband Dominant	1	12
Neither Dominant	2	7
Brother Dominant	1	8

TABLE 37: 7.   Variable 36: Blood Endangers Ritual Objects
(Number of cases: 18)

	Absent	Present
Husband Dominant	1	4
Neither Dominant	2	3
Brother Dominant	2	6

TABLE 38: 7.   Variable 37: Blood Endangers Food Supply
(Number of cases: 21)

	Absent	Present
Husband Dominant	1	6
Neither Dominant	2	6
Brother Dominant	2	4

TABLE 39: 7.   Variable 38: Blood Harms Men
(Number of cases: 22)

	Absent	Present
Husband Dominant	1	9
Neither Dominant	2	3
Brother Dominant	2	5

TABLE 40: 7.   Variable 41: Severity of Sibling Incest Sanctions
(Number of cases: 36)

	1	2	3	4
Husband Dominant	2	2	2	10
Neither Dominant	0	1	2	3
Brother Dominant	0	1	1	12

(1—permitted; 2—no immediate sanctions; 3—mildly punished;
4—severely punished)

TABLE 41: 7.   Variable 42: Nonextension of Incest Taboo
(Number of cases: 44)

	Absent	Sex Relations	Marriage
Husband Dominant	13	2	6
Neither Dominant	6	1	0
Brother Dominant	14	1	1

TABLE 42: 7. Variable 43: Brother-Sister Avoidance
(Number of cases: 52)

	Absent	Total	Partial
Husband Dominant	14	1	8
Neither Dominant	8	1	3
Brother Dominant	9	2	6

TABLE 43: 7. Variable 44: Father-Daughter Avoidance
(Number of cases: 47)

	Absent	Partial
Husband Dominant	18	3
Neither Dominant	11	1
Brother Dominant	11	3

TABLE 44: 7. Variable 45: Intensity of Agriculture
(Number of cases: 64)

	1	2	3	4	5
Husband Dominant	4	4	14	5	2
Neither Dominant	3	0	6	4	1
Brother Dominant	3	0	10	6	2

(1—absent; 2—casual; 3—shifting; 4—horticulture; 5—intensive)

TABLE 45: 7. Variable 46: Intensity of Animal Use
(Number of cases: 64)

	Absent	Present	Intensive
Husband Dominant	7	19	3
Neither Dominant	7	7	0
Brother Dominant	6	14	1

TABLE 46: 7. Variable 47: Intensity of Trade
(Number of cases: 64)

	Absent	Present
Husband Dominant	22	7
Neither Dominant	13	1
Brother Dominant	14	7

TABLE 47: 7. Variable 48: Intensity of Craft Specialization
(Number of cases: 64)

	Absent	Minimal	Extensive
Husband Dominant	16	10	3
Neither Dominant	13	1	0
Brother Dominant	13	5	3

TABLE 48: 7. Variable 49: Social Stratification Scale
(Number of cases: 64)

	Absent	Low	Medium	High
Husband Dominant	15	8	6	0
Neither Dominant	8	1	5	0
Brother Dominant	6	4	9	2

TABLE 49: 7. Variable 50: Political Integration Scale
(Number of cases: 64)

	Minimal	Low	Medium	High
Husband Dominant	16	2	9	2
Neither Dominant	6	3	5	0
Brother Dominant	5	2	13	1

TABLE 50: 7. Variable 51: Spatial Mobility
(Number of cases: 64)

	Low	Medium	High
Husband Dominant	10	11	8
Neither Dominant	5	4	5
Brother Dominant	12	7	2

TABLE 51: 7. Variable 54: Other Residential Types
(Number of cases: 64)

	Absent	Neolocal-ambilocal	Duolocal
Husband Dominant	27	2	0
Neither Dominant	13	1	0
Brother Dominant	17	1	3

8

What the Findings Mean

In this chapter, we shall examine the two groups of variables, reserving for the following chapter a fuller discussion of the three authority patterns and the traits that cluster about them.

INPUTS

The inputs, or features of the societal and community organization that might directly effect the organization of the domestic group, which I included in this study are: societal complexity—including productivity, political integration, and social stratification; spatial mobility; and residence pattern. We shall now review these to see how successful each is as a predictor of domestic authority pattern.

Societal Complexity

Productivity. Three of the variables showed no significant distribution patterns according to domestic authority pattern: intensity of agriculture, intensity of animal use, or intensity of trade (Tables 44: 7, 45: 7, 46: 7). The fourth, however, did: intensity of craft specialization was positively associated with Brother Dominant and Husband Dominant societies as opposed to Neither Dominant societies (Table 18: 7).

The fact is that the great majority of matrilineal societies are in the middle range of productivity and complexity. Of

64 cases for which there was information, 30, or 46.9 percent, practice shifting agriculture, and 15, or 23.4 percent, are horticultural. It is apparent that the mode of cultivation is not by itself an important factor in determining domestic authority. The same is true for intensity of animal use. Out of 64 societies, 40, or 62.5 percent, have domesticated animals present without relying upon them as the major source of diet or income. Given the "middle-range" status of most matrilineal societies, one would not expect many of them to have a complex trade system, and that is the case: for only 15 societies, or 23.4 percent, is intensive trade present.

A better predictor of domestic authority pattern is intensity of craft specialization (Table 18: 7). Presence of specialization is associated with either of the two male dominant types. I am inclined to interpret this as due in part to the large proportion of Neither Dominant societies in North America, which is low on craft specialization. This does not mean, however, that the association is spurious; for in evolutionary terms it may be that there is a greater pull toward male dominance as these nonindustrial societies reach a higher level of productivity. This would depend, I believe, upon the degree to which the domestic unit is a manufacturing unit. In most nonindustrial societies, the domestic unit is the productive unit, but where production is for subsistence only, there is a less pressing need to organize productive activities, for only a limited quantity can be produced with the resources at hand. Where craft specialization is developed, however, skilled labor becomes a valuable asset; and the more the domestic group members can be persuaded or coerced into laboring, the higher the domestic group profits. It would, then, be to the economic advantage of the group to have a strong managerial figure, and one form of male dominance would result.

Political integration. The model portrayed a gradient from minimal to complex political organization going from Type I (extreme husband authority) to Type V (extreme brother authority), with the exception of the Tuareg. On the basis of this, I had predicted that a low level of political complexity would be associated with Husband Dominant societies and a higher level with Brother Dominant.

The first statistical test yielded no significant results, and I concluded that I had divided the cases into too many categories. After collapsing data and retesting, there proved to be a significant association between Brother Dominance and medium to high political integration (Table 20: 7).

I believe that this can be explained by the nature of authority in Brother Dominant societies. Husband Dominance restricts domestic power to the smallest societal unit, the domestic group. This means that the domestic group can act as an autonomous, decision-making unit. This type of domestic authority pattern is adaptive to societies at a low level of social and political integration, where individual family units are likely to splinter off. (I do not imply that Husband Dominance is maladaptive to higher levels of social and political complexity.) Brother Dominance, however, extends decision-making power outside the group for which decisions are being made, from the domestic group of the husband to the wife's brother. There is, therefore, necessary interdependence of domestic groups, with a greater degree of social complexity than is minimally required by Husband Dominance. We would expect a higher level of political integration as a concomitant of the more complex social organization, and that is what the results show.

Social stratification. There is a significant relationship between no or low stratification and Husband Dominant or Neither Dominant domestic authority (Table 19: 7). This pattern emerged from the model where, with the exception of the Tuareg, the Types I, II, and III societies have no stratification, in contrast with Types IV and V, which, with the exception of the Yao, have medium or high stratification.

Little or no stratification is to be expected in middle-range societies. In order to interpret these results, the proper question to ask, then, is why is medium or high stratification present in slightly more than half of Brother Dominant societies in contrast with about a fourth of Husband Dominant and Neither Dominant societies?

This can no doubt be attributed in part to geographic distribution—the high degree of association between Asia and both social stratification and Brother Dominance, and the low degree of association between the Americas and both social stratification and Brother Dominance. However, there may be a functional explanation as well. Brother Dominance extends the cohesiveness of the descent group into the domestic group. A high degree of descent group cohesiveness might be expected when lineages are ranked as corporate units. Therefore, a pull toward Brother Dominance may be one way in which a society responds to social stratification by means of ranked lineages. That it is not the only way is indicated by the presence of Husband Dominance in such states or protostates as Darfur or the Ahaggar drum group (Tuareg).

Spatial Mobility

Spatial mobility shows no significant association with domestic authority pattern (Table 50: 7). The majority of matrilineal societies have medium or low mobility, which is to be expected in primarily middle-range societies with a subsistence base of cultivation.

Residence Patterns

Residence patterns show a high degree of association with domestic authority patterns (Tables 21: 7, 22: 7). As anticipated, virilocality is significantly associated with Husband Dominant, and absence of virilocality is significantly associated with both Brother Dominant and Neither Dominant.

Neither Dominant is strongly matrilocal, with ten out of 14 cases, or 71.4 percent. However, eight Brother Dominant and four Husband Dominant domestic groups also reside matrilocally. One might make a case for the core group of closely related women living together and presenting a united front against the dominance of a male figure, but then one would have to contend with the large number of matrilocal societies with a Brother Dominant pattern. To put it briefly, Neither Dominance is a predictor of matrilocal residence, but matrilocal residence is a predictor of *either* Neither Dominance *or* Brother Dominance.

Brother Dominance shows the greatest amount of diversity of the three domestic authority patterns: eight matrilocal, eight avunculocal, three duolocal,[1] and one each virilocal and neo/ambilocal. The descent-group cohesiveness in Brother Dominant societies is reflected in the two most common residence patterns. Matrilocality unites the related women; and in the societies studied in this sample, there is a strong tendency for the matrilocally residing husbands simply to not be around but rather to spend time in the homes of their mothers and sisters. Avunculocality unites the lineally related men. It is interesting to note that Murdock assumes that the two possibilities in matrilineage or matrisib formation are the localization of the descent group around either a matrilocal core or an avunculocal core (Murdock 1949: 70). While my data do not lead to any hypotheses about descent group origins, it is obvious from the findings that both matrilocal and avunculocal residence are related to the descent group cohesiveness within the domestic group. (In duolocal residence, of course, both men and women of the lineage reside together, increasing even more the cohesiveness of the descent group.)

It can be seen from the discussion above that matrilocality can lead in two directions. It can consist of the lineally related women under the authority of the absentee brother, or it can consist of lineally related women under

---

[1] Duolocal residence is a rare residential form. It is found in only three matrilineal societies—Nayar, Aua, and Minangkabau, all examples of Type V or extreme brother authority. It is also reported in the *Ethnographic Atlas* for the Ga of Africa, possibly matrilineal, and for several nonmatrilineal peoples of Oceania (Murdock 1967). It is possible that duolocality is always associated with strong brother control, whether or not the society is matrilineal. For example, it is discussed as one residential pattern in nineteenth-century Japanese peasant communities (Koyama 1962). Here the eldest brother was head of the resident siblings and the sister's children, who lived all together, and only he could bring his wife and children in to live with him. His sisters had visiting husbands, and his brothers visited their wives at night. This seems to be an example of a Brother Dominant authority pattern, even though descent was bilateral and inheritance patrilineal.

the authority of neither husband nor brother. I cannot agree with Murdock's statement that "it is the woman's superiority to man, especially in production and in the ownership of the principal instrument thereof—land—that favors matrilocal residence" (Murdock 1949: 205). Of the 22 cases of matrilocal residence in the sample, only 10 are Neither Dominant. Therefore, women in societies practicing matrilocal residence have a strong likelihood of being under the authority of a male figure, which is the reverse of Murdock's conclusion.

OUTPUTS

Deference Behavior

The tables show us that deference behavior characterizes Husband Dominant and Brother Dominant societies in contrast to Neither Dominant societies, which appear to be more egalitarian (Tables 1: 7, 2:7). Female to male deference characterizes both of the male dominant societies, while male to male (husband to wife's brother and vice versa) deference characterizes very few. Of the total sample, one or both forms of female deference characterize 34 societies, or 51.5 percent. Taking only those societies for which there are data on female deference, the percentage of cases in which it is present rises to 64.2 percent. So much for woman's high status in matrilineal societies.

An interesting finding is that there appears to be a tendency, albeit a weak one, for Brother Dominant societies to exhibit husband-to-wife's brother deference (Variable 7). Does this indicate that bride givers are superior to bride takers? Recalling Leach's contention that matrilateral cross-cousin marriage serves to maintain a distinction in rank between intermarrying lineages (Leach 1951), I examined the societies exhibiting this deference pattern for indications of unilateral cross-cousin marriage. Of the eight societies for which husband-to-wife's brother deference was present, four had no preference, three preferred the patrilateral form, and only one (Nayar) preferred the matrilateral form. Deference of the husband to the wife's brother, therefore, seems to relate to the internal organization of the domestic group rather than to lineage status.

Control Over Person

These variables show a high degree of association with the authority patterns. This is to be expected, as authority is, after all, legitimate power over the actions of others.

My assumption was that marriage rituals can be viewed as a rite of passage establishing and symbolizing the relationship of husband and wife in the marriage. This has been supported, particularly for Husband Dominant societies, in which the marriage ceremony marks the change of authority over the woman from her natal domestic group to her husband (Table 3: 7, Variables 9 and 12).

Disruption of marriage and divorce are also closely associated with the authority patterns (Tables 4: 7, 5: 7). In both Brother Dominant and Neither Dominant societies, the stable figure tends to be the woman, with the husband leaving in case of divorce. This is readily comprehensible in the case of matrilineal societies, where the core of the descent group is the woman and her children, incorporating the key dyads of mother-child, sister-sister, brother-brother, and brother-sister.

The aggression variables (Tables 6: 7, 7: 7) are akin to the deference variables. While women in Husband Dominant societies tend to defer only to the husband and stand under threat of aggression from him alone, women in Brother Dominant societies tend to owe deference to both husband and brother and are under threat of sanction from both. This implies that the matrilineal puzzle is especially keen for women in Brother Dominant societies. On the other hand, the man in the Brother Dominant society is in a strong position, with two categories of women to turn to for support. One wonders why there are not more Brother Dominant societies—or if there are more that have gone unrecognized by ethnographers.

I assumed that control over children would follow automatically from control over their mothers. I was wrong. There is a strong association between control patterns and authority patterns, but it is not tautological (Table 8: 7). This problem will be discussed further in the chapters on cross-cousin marriage (Chapter 10) and the incest taboo (Chapter 11).

Control Over Property

Again, the association is strong between authority patterns and control over domestic group property. A look at the data (Table 9: 7) will show that this variable can be plotted along a gradient paralleling the domestic authority gradient. This will become clearer if we collapse some of the categories:

TABLE 1: 8. Property Control (Revised)

	Husband Control	Female Participation	Brother Control
Husband Dominant	16	7	—
Neither Dominant	—	14	—
Brother Dominant	—	8	9

$\chi^2 = 49.20$ $p < .001$ $C = .70$

(Husband Control—total control by the Husband; Female Participation—total female control or control shared with husband or brother; Brother Control—total brother control.) I leave out the three cases of control shared between husband and brother: Ashanti, Trobriand Islands, and Tsimshian. There were two cases in the category "brother and sister share control," Khasi and Nauru. I put Khasi under Brother Control, because the brother is the manager of the property even though it is legally in his sister's name; and I put Nauru under Female Participation (as a case of "woman control"), because it is the eldest sister who has the greatest authority over the land.

Of all the variables, then, control over property is the one most clearly and strongly associated with domestic group authority. The varied implications of this relationship are obvious: causality could go in either direction, from economic control to group authority or vice versa, or both could be a response to a third factor or regression of factors. My data can give no support to any causal theory: this would require structural and historical investigations of several representative cases. The data do show that there is the possibility for a smooth transition from any one of the total control types—Husband, Woman, or Brother—to either of the other two by going through a shared type—Husband-Wife, Brother-Sister, or Husband-Brother. By this I do not imply that the shared types are only transitional in nature; on the contrary, they can be stable types, with spheres of economic control between partners clearly defined and well integrated into other aspects of social organization. Trobriand Islands domestic economy is a good example. The husband-brother economic relationship is an important feature of the political organization, as the chief receives goods from the brothers of his wives (as do all men). Since it is only aristocrats who are polygynous, this gives the chief an economic advantage and expedites the redistributive system.

Female Autonomy

All of the variables directly associated with the domestic group show a significant distribution, with the exception of polyandry (Table 27: 7), adultery allowed for the husband (Table 28: 7), and adultery allowed for the wife (Table 29: 7).

Plural marriage. The results of the tests were, for the most part, in the predicted directions (Tables 10: 7, 11: 7). Polygyny is more often absent in Neither Dominant societies and more often present in male dominant societies than would be expected by chance. General polygyny is strongly associated with Husband Dominance. Where polygyny is present in Neither Dominant societies, sororal polygyny is either preferred or permitted in the societies for which there are data. This indicates that women in Neither Dominant societies are relatively free from sexual competition within the home, as they tend to share their husbands

either with no one or with a sister. It is interesting to ob-
serve that there tends to be a preference against sororal
polygyny in Brother Dominant societies: apparently men
prefer to distribute their social resources—their sisters—
broadly in creating brother-in-law ties. Women in Husband
Dominant societies, on the other hand, may suffer from
sexual competition (Table 11: 7), and this is reflected in
the findings on co-wife jealousy (Table 12: 7).

I had assumed that polyandry would show significant
associations with domestic group patterns, as it could allow
the wife to play one husband against the other and thereby
improve her position in regard to all. The absence of significant findings can perhaps be accounted for by the fact
that, except for the Nayar, polyandrous unions are the exception rather than the common or preferred form of marriage.

Sexual restrictions. The tests concerning the punishment of
the wife's adultery (Table 13: 7) and the right of the husband to dispose of his wife's sexuality (Variable 27)
yielded significant results in the predicted direction. However, there was no significant association between authority
patterns and the allowing of adultery for either husband or
wife (Tables 28: 7, 29: 7). The noteworthy fact in these
tables is that almost double the percentage allow adultery
for the husband (60 percent) as allow it for the wife (32.1
percent), in spite of the fact that children resulting from an
adulterous union belong to their mother's descent group
and are not, therefore, cuckoos in the father's lineal nest. It
is hard to explain why wives should be expected to be
sexually faithful so much more often than husbands. I can
think of no biological or psychological reason for this, and
the usual structural explanation of the child's membership
in his father's descent group is not valid for matrilineal
societies. Could it be that women are somehow *less* monogamous than men and therefore need stronger controls?
This is certainly an ancient assumption in Western thought,
dating at least as far back in time as the early fathers of
the Church, who saw woman as Eve the Temptress. But

this hypothesis is as hard to take seriously as its reverse, the common assumption in our society that women are more monogamous than men. If that were so, there would be no need for more frequent sanctions against women's adultery.

One possibility suggests itself, which is that the wife's adultery is forbidden or frowned upon because it tends to disrupt the in-law bond between husband and brother, regardless of who is in authority over the woman or whether either is; and the frequency of this negative sanction is due to the frequency with which this in-law bond is structurally important to the society beyond the domestic group. I know of no societies in which the in-law relationship between women equals or supersedes in importance that between men. The female in-law bond, of course, may be unreported, because no one thought to look for it. Nevertheless, the fact remains that the brother-in-law bond can be a very critical one in economic or political relationships—to recognize this, one has only to consider the case of the Trobriand Islanders reviewed above.

Those variables relating to female autonomy not directly associated with the domestic group were more disappointing. Only one significant association resulted from the tests of social positions and menstrual restrictions.

Social positions. I have already indicated my dissatisfaction with the data on social positions of women (Chapter 2). Of the five variables concerning women's participation in community or societal activities, only one (Table 14: 7) showed significant distribution.

Menstrual restrictions. None of the variables relating to menstrual restrictions showed any association with the domestic authority patterns. This finding contrasts with those of Young and Bacdayan (1965, cited in Chapter 2) that menstrual restrictions are related to male dominance. Leaving aside the question of the trustworthiness of their findings, this contrast calls for some comment.

First, I have already observed that the data on menstrual restrictions may be suspect: with one exception, the Hopi, for which I was the ethnographer, only the presence, but not the absence, of menstrual taboos is reported. We cannot assume that this is representative.

Second, the notion that menstruation disadvantages women may be characteristic mainly of Western societies, along with a few others—such as India and the Semitic groups—which regard the menstruating woman as ritually unclean. While the notion that the menstruating woman may be dangerous to others and perhaps to herself is not uncommon, this is not necessarily associated with feelings of uncleanliness or inferiority. That this may be true even in societies practicing menstrual seclusion is illustrated by the Kaska:

> Sexual intercourse with a menstruant caused a man to pass blood in his urine so that he would sicken and die. Despite this belief boys seized on the easy accessibility of girls in seclusion who, in turn, did not always resist their advances. When they became ill the youths might confess such offenses [Honigman 1954: 124].

It is the blood itself, not the woman, that is dangerous: modern Kaska youths practice intercourse with menstruating girls, protecting themselves from contact with the blood through the use of condoms (Honigman 1949: 162).

Third, there are striking parallels, especially in American Indian practices, between restrictions placed upon menstruating women and men in a state of spiritual tension or danger, such as before warfare or the hunt, after homicide, or during ceremonial periods. Whether this is true on a worldwide basis I am not prepared to say. I believe that the suggestion merits research. I hypothesize that practices concerning menstruation are a subclass of practices concerning a state of spiritual danger, and that tests of association and geographical distribution would show this to be the case.
Cross-cousin marriage and sibling incest. These sets of variables will be discussed in Chapters 10 and 11.

Avoidance

The tests yielded nonsignificant results (Tables 42: 7, 43: 7), and neither of my hypotheses concerning brother-sister avoidance has been confirmed, nor has that concerning father-daughter avoidance. However, the fact that 40.4 percent of the societies in the sample do practice brother-sister avoidance might prove to be significant if matrilineal societies were compared with nonmatrilineal ones. If so, it would indicate that sibling avoidance was an extension of descent-group principles into the domestic group.

The fact that the results on the sibling-avoidance test do not follow the direction of the two variables testing for incest taboos leads me to conclude that the avoidance is not necessarily a device for enforcing the sibling incest taboo. If it were, we could logically expect that Brother Dominant societies would have either relatively strong avoidance rules, as a means of enforcing the taboo, or relatively weak ones, because the taboo would be so strongly internalized.

Father-daughter avoidance exists, but with my data I cannot relate it to any other feature. Thinking that it might be an extension of female respect behavior, I tested this variable in relation to Variable 5: Wife Defers to Husband, with no significant results. Nor was there any association with residence patterns.

With the data I have, I can only say the following: (a) father-daughter avoidance does exist (b) matrilineal societies *may* tend more than others to practice brother-sister avoidance, and (c) there is no evidence to support the notion that sibling avoidance behavior exists to enforce the incest taboo.

In this chapter, I have presented interpretations for the findings of the statistical tests. I would like now to say a few words regarding these interpretations.

As to Inputs, it is clear that neither the mode of production per se nor the pattern of spatial mobility connected with it has any significant association with the domestic authority pattern. The organization of the domestic group is much more clearly tied to organizational features in production, as revealed by the association between male authority and intensive craft specialization.

I have given functional explanations for the association between Brother Dominance and both medium-to-high political integration and medium-to-high stratification. I do not, however, find these explanations entirely satisfactory: I feel that an equally plausible explanation is the fact that there is a strong association between Brother Dominance and geographic location in Asia, an area of complex traditional cultures. Therefore, we cannot overlook the possibility that these are spurious functional associations.

The residence pattern is the area in which community organization most clearly overlaps with domestic group organization. Here, as we might expect, there is a strong association between domestic authority and residence rules.

The Outputs show a high degree of correlation, as predicted, with the domestic authority types. This fact indicates to me that the authority types as I have defined them are meaningful classes of attitudes and behavior, and not merely nominal classes.

It has been demonstrated that female autonomy varies according to domestic authority, where the internal organization of the domestic group is concerned. However, female autonomy does not necessarily increase in matters going beyond the domestic group with a decrease in domestic control over women—with one exception: the presence or absence of ascribed positions open only to women. That is, we cannot assume that greater autonomy in the home *necessarily* correlates with high status in the broader sociocultural sphere.

Greater autonomy in the home does not necessarily mean that women can carry their sexual activities outside the domestic group in approved or allowed adultrous affairs. This restriction on personal expression of sexual desires surprised me, and I asked myself what stake the society at large would have in forbidding or disapproving female adultery. I concluded that this disruption of the domestic group would disrupt affinal relationships, notably that between brothers-in-law, which in many societies is a very important achieved relationship. While adultery on the part of the husband might disrupt the relationship between sisters-in-law, this is rarely an important structural dyad within the framework of the larger society.

Greater control over her own person does not give a woman freedom from menstrual restrictions. I think we can safely put to rest the hoary notion that menstrual restrictions indicate low female status, or any status position whatsoever. If we think of the nature of menstrual taboos and how similar they are to restrictions applied by many cultures to disruptions of normal physical or spiritual status, such as death, killing in warfare or the chase, ceremonial activities, and the like, it appears that menstrual restrictions are of the same nature and differ only in being automatic and periodic. It may be that some cultures have used menstruation to explain and justify the inferior status of women; but that is a culture-specific trait and cannot be generalized to all cultures having menstrual taboos.[2]

The findings on avoidance behavior were a disappointment. Obviously, avoidance is the most effective means of establishing distance between individuals. However, this seems not to be of the same nature as the distance established by the incest taboos (see Chapter 11) or female deference.

In the next chapter, I shall discuss how these traits cluster around the domestic authority patterns into what I have called authority pattern syndromes.

---

[2] Since doing the research for this study, I have received further information on Hopi attitudes toward menstruation. The feeling exists with some people that sexual relations may be harmful to the woman, even though at this time she is more sexually attractive to men than when she is not menstruating. However, not everyone holds this attitude. It is likely that there was a taboo which is breaking down.

9

Matrilineal Domestic Group Profiles

SIX POSSIBILITIES

In the preceding chapter we examined the results of the statistical tests. We found that certain traits are associated strongly or significantly with a single authority pattern. Others are associated strongly or significantly with two patterns, in contrast to their lack of association with the third. These associations are illustrated in Figure 4.

To recapitulate briefly, my major hypothesis is that there are three types of authority patterns: Husband Dominance, Brother Dominance and Neither Dominance. By playing the three authority patterns against the two sexual dominance patterns—i.e. male dominant versus nonmale dominant—we arrive at six possible types, the three "pure" types and the three "mixed" types. In this chapter, I shall discuss the "pure" types and the "mixed" type of Husband Dominant combined with Brother Dominant. As one can see from examining Figure 4, the other "mixed" types, Neither Dominant combined with Husband Dominant and Neither Dominant combined with Brother Dominant, contain only two variables each and do not constitute syndromes of traits. I shall also discuss the results of a trio of factor analyses which corroborate the logical analysis.

Husband Dominant

As we might expect, associated with Husband Dominance are those traits which define the husband's authority over

FIGURE 4: Trait Distribution by Type

Traits Strongly or Significantly Associated With One Type

Husband Dominant	Neither Dominant	Brother Dominant
Bride capture	No preference against sororal polygyny	Husband defers to wife's brother
Husband controls property.	Ascribed positions exclusive to women	Brother controls property
Husband punishes wife's adultery	Absence of cross-cousin marriage preference	Brother punishes sister's adultery
Father-daughter incest worse	Absence of traits shared by Husband Dominant and Brother Dominant	Brother-sister incest worse
Preference for matrilateral cross-cousin marriage		Preference for patrilateral cross-cousin marriage
Virilocality		Medium-high stratification
Substantial bridewealth		Mother's brother controls children
Woman exchange		Brother aggression allowed
Divorce: wife leaves		Wife's brother disrupts marriage
Co-wife jealousy		Sister defers to brother
Husband disposes of wife's sexuality		

Shared Traits

Husband Dominant and Neither Dominant: Father control of children
Minimal-low stratification

Neither Dominant and Brother Dominant: Divorce: husband leaves
Sibling incest taboos extended

Husband Dominant and Brother Dominant: Wife defers to husband
Husband aggression allowed
Male control of property
Polygyny
Wife's adultery punished
Craft specialization

his wife and give it recognition. The three wedding customs that indicate ownership through capture or purchase are found in significant association with this type. Residence tends to be virilocal; i.e. it is the bride who disrupts her natal ties to join her affinal group; and if divorce occurs, it tends to be she who must make the physical break and leave the home.

Ownership of rights to the wife's sexuality by the husband is strongly associated with this authority pattern: it is only with this type that the husband can dispose of his wife's sexuality to others, and the right of the husband to punish adultery committed by his wife is significantly associated with this type.

The relatively large number of cases in which the husband has control over domestic group property (16, or 27.6 percent of the sample of 58 societies) are exclusively Husband Dominant. This tells us that in Husband Dominant societies, the husband tends to control not only the person of his wife but also the material goods upon which she depends.

It is interesting to note that co-wife jealousy is significantly associated with this authority type. Of the cases coded Husband Dominant, 70 percent have co-wife jealousy reported "present," compared with 30 percent of Neither Dominant and 33.3 percent of Brother Dominant societies. This association leads me to conclude that dependence of the wife upon the husband is a corollary of husband authority over the wife, so that competition threatens the wife's security with this authority pattern more than it does with the other patterns (see also the discussion in Chapter 11). This conclusion, in turn, casts doubt upon the widely held notion that the woman in matrilineal societies, because she is a central figure in her descent group, is relatively independent of her husband. What these findings suggest is that the critical factor is not the descent system per se but rather the organization of the domestic group. (Without comparing matrilineal societies to other societies, we cannot at this point determine whether husband authority is less severe in Husband Dominant matrilineal societies than in nonmatrilineal societies. Several of the ethnographers who were consulted for this study implied that matrilineality tempers the authority of the husband.)

There are two other variables that are found to be significantly associated with the husband authority pattern: preference for matrilateral cross-cousin marriage and the notion that father-daughter incest is worse than sibling incest. I reserve comment upon these for later chapters.

Brother Dominant

This authority pattern is clearly associated with the right of the brother to interfere in the domestic group of his adult, married sister, where he is not the leading male member of it (as with duolocal residence). Wife's brother disrupts marriage to a significant degree; and there is a significant tendency for the brother to punish his sister's adultery. There may be a tendency for the husband to defer to the wife's brother more with this authority pattern than with the others.

Brothers are more likely to punish adult sisters in societies with this authority pattern. They are more likely to control the property used by their married sisters: this is true for seven, or 35 percent, of the Brother Dominant cases with data on property control.

The woman's brother exerts significantly greater control over her minor children in Brother Dominant societies than in the other two types. This leads me to conclude that the "matrilineal puzzle" for the growing boy must be greater in the Husband Dominant and Neither Dominant domestic groups with father control, for the boy must transfer his dependence and loyalty from his father to his mother's brother as he matures. A problem for future investigation might be a study of the mechanisms by which this is accomplished.

There is a significant relationship between Brother Dominance and medium-to-high social stratification. This has been discussed in Chapter 8.

As predicted, there is a significant association between Brother Dominance and: (a) preference for patrilateral cross-cousin marriage, and (b) the notion that sibling incest is worse than father-daughter incest. These will be discussed in later chapters.

Husband Dominant and Brother Dominant

The most parsimonious way of characterizing the variables that are shared by the two male dominant patterns is to consider them indications of just that—male dominance.

The wife defers to her husband. She is likely to be subjected to husband aggression as I have defined it. Male control of property is present to a significant degree. Wife's adultery is punished. In contrast to Neither Dominant, the woman in one of the two male dominant patterns has a lesser degree of control over her person and property.

Polygyny is also strongly associated with male authority. While this could be readily explained for Husband Dominance as advantageous to the husband, it is not so easy to explain for Brother Dominance. There are two interpretations which occur to me: (a) polygyny is a marker of depressed female status, and (b) polygyny is adaptive to the middle level of productivity that characterizes most matrilineal societies, in which case polygyny would be "normal" and the feature to be explained would be rather the relative absence of polygyny in Neither Dominant societies.

Craft specialization also tends to be characteristic of male dominant societies in contrast to Neither Dominant ones. This has been discussed in the preceding chapter.

Neither Dominant

Neither Dominant domestic groups appear to be characterized more by the absence of traits associated with, or shared by, Husband Dominant and Brother Dominant domestic groups than by the significant presence of traits coded for in this study. Only two variables are significantly "present" for this authority pattern: matrilocality and ascribed positions exclusive to women. This does not, however, mean that Neither Dominant is a residual category. The important point here is that in Neither Dominant domestic groups, women have greater control over their persons—both as to control over their sexuality and freedom from husband aggression—than do women under the other authority patterns. They also have a greater share in control over property: there are no cases of exclusive male control in the Neither Dominant group. Matrilocality gives women the advantage of uniting natal with marital households. The proportionately larger number of societies granting women exclusive ascribed positions means that along with this type of domestic authority pattern goes a greater assurance of important positions in the society outside the home. In other words, where women are more independent at home, they tend to be more important in the society at large. (However, on this point see page 92.)

From the information given above, it is clear that there are three distinct authority patterns for matrilineal domestic groups. The material supports the hypothesis given by Lévi-Strauss (1963), that where the relationship between husband and wife is strong, that between brother and sister will tend to be weak, and vice versa. (Unlike Lévi-Strauss, I am not concerned with feelings of hostility or affection.) However, he overlooked the possibility of neither the husband nor the brother having a stronger relationship with the woman than the other. I find that this can be the case.

The second major hypothesis, concerning the nature of power in the domestic group, was that where power was not concentrated it decreased in quantity. This hypothesis has also been confirmed. Husband Dominant and Brother Dominant types combine, crossing the tripartite distinction with a two-fold one. The traits shared by Husband Dominant and Brother Dominant indicate general male authority over women in these societies. Neither Dominant, by its absence of these traits and the presence of matrilocality and ascribed societal positions exclusive to women, is an organizational pattern which allows for a high degree of female autonomy, or control of the adult married woman over her person and property, and grants her positions of some importance outside the domestic group.

FACTOR ANALYSES

In order to test the validity of the logical constructs, I subjected the variables to a series of factor analyses.

Factor analysis refers to procedures devised to analyze the intercorrelations within a set of variables (Cooley and Lohnes 1962: Chapter 8). By using factor analyses, I hoped to answer the following questions:

1. When all variables are being tested in relation to all others, as they are in tests for intercorrelation, will the au-

thority patterns, constructed on the bases of logic and the findings of the probability tests, emerge as significant loci for clusters of variables? I predicted that they would, that the variables associated significantly with each authority pattern would intercorrelate more highly with one another than with other variables.

2. What are the variables that intercorrelate to the highest degree, accounting for the most variance within the total group of variables?

3. Within each cluster, which variables account for the highest degree of positive or negative intercorrelation? (This is asking what traits, by their presence or absence, are the most important in "pulling together" the cluster.)

4. What factor can be identified as the underlying variable—whether one of the variables present in the cluster or an unnamed, "lurking" variable—which best encompasses the entire cluster? For example, in Test 1, I identify the factor in the Factor I cluster as "High Female Autonomy," even though that is not a variable in the cluster; and in the same test, I identify the underlying factor in the Factor II cluster as Brother Dominance, which is one of the variables in the cluster.

I subjected the variables to a series of three factor analyses, using different combinations of variables for each of the tests. I selected the 30 strong or significant variables for which there was information on 40 or more cases, plus the three authority patterns and five world areas (Figure 5). I instructed the computer to sort the data into five clusters, to allow for the three authority patterns to emerge and to take care of "noise," or variables that would not intercorrelate strongly with any of the others. I was prepared to have different factors than authority patterns arise.

FIGURE 5: Factor Analyses Variables

1. Husband Dominant
2. Neither Dominant
3. Brother Dominant
4. Wife defers to husband
5. Bride capture
6. Substantial bridewealth

7. Woman exchange
8. Divorce—wife leaves
9. Divorce—husband leaves
10. Wife's brother disrupts marriage
11. Husband aggression allowed
12. Father controls children
13. Mother's brother controls children
14. Male control of property
15. Husband controls property
16. Brother controls property
17. Polygyny
18. Co-wife jealousy
19. Polyandry
20. Wife's adultery punished
21. Adultery punished by husband
22. Adultery punished by brother
23. Women hold ascribed exclusive positions
24. Preference for matrilateral cross-cousin marriage
25. Preference for patrilateral cross-cousin marriage
26. Sibling incest restrictions broadly extended
27. Craft specialization
28. Minimal-low stratification
29. Medium-high stratification
30. Low spatial mobility
31. Matrilocality
32. Avunculocality
33. Virilocality
34. Africa
35. Asia
36. Oceania
37. South America
38. North America

Test 1: Variables 1-33

This test included the 30 variables plus the three authority patterns.

Factor I. This factor, which accounted for 15.5 percent of the variance, showed a high loading—i.e. .500 or higher—for 10 traits. Those variables positively intercorrelated with this factor are: 9—Husband leaves after divorce; 23—Women hold positions; and 31—Matrilocality. The variables negatively intercorrelated are: 8—Wife leaves after divorce; 11—Husband aggression allowed; 14—Male control of property; 15—Husband controls property; 20—Wife's adultery punished; 21—Adultery punished by husband; and 33—Virilocality. A slightly lower loading, .453, arises for variable 2—Neither Dominant.

The variables with the highest loadings are those related to matrilocal residence, absence of punishment of the wife, and positions held outside the home (variables 8, 9, 20, 23, and 31). These all point in the direction of the woman's control of herself and her milieu. Therefore, I call this factor *High Female Autonomy*.

Factor II. This factor, which accounts for 14.8 percent of the variance in this test, shows seven traits with high loadings. Those positively intercorrelated with this factor are: 3—Brother Dominant; 10—Wife's brother disrupts marriage; 13—Mother's brother controls children; 16—Brother controls property; and 22—Adultery punished by brother. Those negatively intercorrelated with this factor are: 1—Husband Dominant; and 12—Father controls children. I call this factor *Brother Dominance*, because Variable 3, Brother Dominant, has the highest loading.

Factor III. This factor, which accounts for 9.1 percent of the variance, shows three traits highly intercorrelated. Variable 2—Neither Dominant, is positively intercorrelated; and Variable 4—Wife defers to husband, and Variable 27—Craft specialization, are negatively intercorrelated. In addition, there are weaker loadings, in the .300-.499 range, of Polyandry (positive), Substantial bridewealth (negative), Male control of property (negative), and Husband control of property (negative) with this factor. I call this factor *Neither Dominance*, because Neither Dominant (Variable 2) is one of the two variables with highest loading, the other being the absence of Wife Defers to Husband (Variable 4).

Factor IV. The only high loadings for this factor, which accounts for 8.6 percent of the variance, are: Variable 28—Minimal-low stratification (negative); and Variable 29—Medium-high stratification (positive).

Factor V. This factor, accounting for 8.3 percent of the variance, has three variables with high positive loadings: Variable 7—Woman exchange; Variable 17—Polygyny; and Variable 18—Co-wife jealousy. There is also a weak loading for Variable 1—Husband Dominant. The variables with high loading in this cluster are those which characterize either Husband Dominant or Husband and Brother Dominant, and are evidence of male control. Therefore, I consider this factor to be *Low Female Autonomy.* The two importance factors in this test are *High Female Autonomy* and *Brother Dominance.*

Test 2: Variables 1-38

This test consisted of the 30 variables, the three authority patterns, and the five world areas.

Factor I. There are nine variables with high loadings in this factor, which accounts for 15.6 percent of the variance. Those positively intercorrelated are: Variable 2—Neither Dominant; Variable 9—Husband leaves after divorce; Variable 31—Matrilocality. Those negatively intercorrelated are: Variable 8—Wife leaves after divorce; Variable 11—Husband aggression; Variable 14—Male control of property; Variable 17—Polygyny; Variable 20—Wife's adultery punished; and Variable 21—Adultery punished by husband. In addition, Variable 35—Asia, has a lesser loading (.447). There are two interpretations for this factor: *Neither Dominant* and *High Female Autonomy.*

If Neither Dominant (Variable 2) had had a higher loading, I would have considered this to be the underlying factor. As it was, there were six variables with higher loading. As these all point in the direction of absence of male control over the woman, I am inclined to consider the factor to be Neither Dominant. The ambiguity reflects the close relationship between Neither Dominance and freedom from any male control.

Factor II. This factor, which accounts for 13.9 percent of the variance, has six variables that are highly intercorrelated. Those positively intercorrelated are: Variable 3—Brother Dominant; Variable 10—Wife's brother disrupts marriage; Variable 13—Mother's brother controls children; Variable 16—Brother controls property; and Variable 22—Adultery punished by brother. The one negatively intercorrelated is Variable 12—Father controls children. In addition, Variable 35—Asia, has a weak loading (.338). I call this factor *Brother Dominance*, because Brother Dominant (Variable 3) has the highest loading.

Factor III. The stratification variables again emerge as the only ones highly intercorrelated with this factor, which accounts for 8.2 percent of the variance.

Factor IV. Accounting for 7.8 percent of the variance, this factor has only two variables highly intercorrelated: Variable 24—Matrilateral cross-cousin marriage preferred (negative); and Variable 38—North America (positive). There is a lesser positive loading (.409) for Neither Dominant. I consider this factor to be *North America*, as it best accounts for the three variables.

Factor V. This factor, which accounts for 7.3 percent of the variance, has four variables which are highly intercorrelated. There are positive loadings for: Variable 4—Wife defers to husband; Variable 27—Craft specialization; and Variable 34—Africa. There is a negative loading for Variable 19—Polyandry. There is also a weak loading (.363) for Variable 1—Husband Dominant. I call this factor *Africa*, as it has the highest loading.

I had expected there to be a stronger relationship between world areas and authority types; but the only world areas with distinctive authority patterns within matrilineal societies appear to be North America—which is associated with Neither Dominant domestic groups—and Africa—which is associated with Husband Dominant domestic groups. If I had included a variable "Male Dominance," it is likely that both Africa and Oceania would have been highly correlated with this variable.

Test 3: Variables 4-33

The elimination of the three authority patterns and the world areas as variables in this test yielded results that differed from but complemented the two preceding test results.

Factor I. This factor, accounting for 15.7 percent of the variance, shows a high positive intercorrelation of five variables: Variable 8—Wife leaves after divorce; Variable 14—Male control of property; Variable 15—Husband control of property; Variable 21—Adultery punished by husband; and Variable 33—Virilocality. Two variables show a high negative intercorrelation: Variable 9—Husband leaves after divorce; and Variable 31—Matrilocality.

The variables with the highest loading (Variables 8, 15, 33) are all highly associated with the husband authority pattern. Therefore, I consider the factor to be *Husband Dominance.*

Factor II. This factor, which accounts for 11.9 percent of the variance, has seven variables, all positive, highly intercorrelated: Variable 4—Wife defers to husband; Variable 10—Wife's brother disrupts marriage; Variable 11—Husband aggression; Variable 17—Polygyny; Variable 20—Wife's adultery punished; Variable 21—Husband punishes adultery; and Variable 32—Avunculocality.

These variables all point away from the woman's control over her person and her marriage. Therefore, I call this factor *Low Female Autonomy.*

Factor III again shows high intercorrelation of the two stratification variables. The other two groupings seem to be residual categories, with no clearly overriding factors.

Taken together, the three factor analysis tests corroborate the findings of the chi square tests.

1. There are three distinct authority patterns. I have identified Brother Dominance as Factor II in Test 1, and Factor II in Test 2. Neither Dominance is Factor III in Test 1, and possibly Factor I in Test 2. Husband Dominance is Factor I in Test 3.

2. Crosscutting the authority patterns is a division into high and low female autonomy. I have identified as High Female Autonomy Factor I of Test 1 and possibly Factor I of Test 2. My indecision as to the identification of Factor I of Test 2, whether to consider it Neither Dominant or High Female Autonomy, is a reflection of the close association of these two traits. Factor V of Test 1 and Factor II of Test 3 are identified as Low Female Autonomy.

In addition to the intercorrelations I had predicted, there are two factors which can best be identified as world areas, Factors IV and V of Test 2, North America and Africa, respectively. However, world area did not come out as the most important variable: in Test 2, which was a test for the importance of world area, the strongest factors are Brother Dominant and the ambiguous factor identified as either Neither Dominant or High Female Autonomy.

The congruence between the bivariate analyses (the chi square tests) and the multivariate analyses (the factor tests) is unlikely to have occurred by chance. This gives me confidence that the two theorems, or major hypotheses, that have been presented in the Introduction have been confirmed:

1. The model represents a true picture of domestic organization in the universe of matrilineal societies. These societies are codeable into the five domestic authority patterns. Furthermore, as the two kinds of analyses, bivariate and multivariate, have demonstrated, there are statistically significant clusters of variables, or trait syndromes, associated with each of the dominance patterns.

2. When authority over the woman disperses, the autonomy, or freedom of action, of the woman increases. The Neither Dominant category is strongly associated with the variables related to high female autonomy, while women under the authority of either husband or brother tend to have much less control over person and property and a less significant role in broader societal activities.

In the next two chapters, I shall discuss the findings related to the two hypotheses I presented in the Introduction, regarding the relationship between domestic authority and cross-cousin marriage, and domestic authority and the direction of the incest taboo.

10

Domestic Authority and Unilateral Cross-Cousin Marriage

All appearances to the contrary nonwithstanding, the subject of unilateral cross-cousin marriage has not been beaten to death. In this chapter, once again it raises its head.

It would require a paper of considerable length to detail the controversy begun by Homans and Schneider's "psychological" rejoinder (1955) to Lévi-Strauss's "structural" statement of cross-cousin marriage rules. That is not the purpose of this chapter, which will attempt to show that Homans and Schneider were right, but for the wrong reasons. However, some comments on the history of the controversy are in order.

In his book *Les Structures Elémentaires de la Parenté* (1949), Lévi-Strauss hypothesized that a preference for matrilateral cross-cousin marriage is much more common than a preference for patrilateral cross-cousin marriage, because the former necessarily involves greater dependence of kin groups upon one another, through indirect exchange, than does the latter; and, thereby, the former generates greater organic solidarity. Strongly implied, although not stated, is the notion that organic solidarity and its benefits are self-evident, and that these benefits account for the adoption, in the majority of societies in which unilateral cross-cousin marriage exists, of the matrilateral over the patrilateral form.

Homans and Schneider took issue with this position in their book *Marriage, Authority, and Final Causes* (1955). They make three major points: (a) Lévi-Strauss was wrong in assuming that patrilateral cross-cousin marriage created less organic solidarity than the matrilateral form: the patrilateral form requires reciprocity in alternate generations and, therefore, necessitates as much or more interdependence (Homans and Schneider 1955: 13); (b) Lévi-Strauss neglects to show how marriage preferences actually come about; and (c) once the process of deciding the preference, their "efficient cause," is shown, the theory Lévi-Strauss proposes becomes unnecessary.

Beginning with the implied premise that people tend to act in accordance with what they perceive as their own best interest, Homans and Schneider ask on what basis the choice of preference is made. (Like Lévi-Strauss, they remain in the realm of rules and are not talking about actual marriage decisions.) Asking on what basis the choice of preference is made, they take the position that choice of spouse is in accord with the structure of sentiment within the kin group of Ego, the bride-seeker. They hypothesize that one's choice of spouse depends upon one's choice of in-law; that is, where one prefers one's father, one likes his sister and selects her for mother-in-law (patrilateral cross-cousin marriage), and where one prefers one's mother, one likes her brother and selects him for father-in-law (the matrilateral form). The basis for this hypothesis is the principle of sentiment extension proposed by Radcliffe-Brown: Sentimental equivalence of siblings follows from their structural equivalence, so that where one parent is regarded as kind and indulgent, that parent's siblings will also be looked upon in this way (Radcliffe-Brown 1952).

The next step in their analysis is to examine societies having cross-cousin marriage preference, and to test the fit between form of preference and sentiment type. The authors assume that in patrilineal societies the father is stern and the mother indulgent; therefore, according to the reasoning above, the matrilateral form is most sentimentally appropriate. Conversely, in matrilineal societies, the mother's brother is stern and the father indulgent, making the patrilateral form sentimentally appropriate. They tested the patrilateral form against the matrilateral form for matrilineal descent versus patrilineal descent on 36 societies for which they found a preference stated. Their findings were highly significant: $p = .009$. If one accepts their sample, then there is no question of the association of matrilateral cross-cousin marriage with patrilineal descent and patrilateral cross-cousin marriage with matrilineal descent. Unfortunately, their sample violates the strictures that have been proposed for cross-cultural sample construction since the publication of their book. However, the high degree of significance of the findings, and the general agreement of those familiar with the literature on marriage, support their results.

The authors believe that their hypothesis of sentimental appropriateness has been confirmed. They also believe that the greater number of matrilateral cases over patrilateral cases is best explained by the greater number of patrilineal over matrilineal descent systems. This, they feel, does not make Lévi-Strauss's hypothesis wrong, but simply unnecessary.

At this point Needham came to the attack, and to Lévi-Strauss's defense, in *Structure and Sentiment* (1962). It would be superfluous to recapitulate his criticism, or to answer it: this has been done by Ackerman (1964), Coult (1962), Harris (1968), and Lévi-Strauss himself (1969). The controversy seems by now to have subsided. By picking it up, I do not intend to get embroiled in structural explanations in opposition to psychological ones—surely they are complementary rather than contradictory; I merely want to use this well-trodden path as a testing ground for a theory of my own.

While matrilateral cross-cousin marriage admits of readily comprehensible explanations—the role of the mother's brother having been understood at least since Radcliffe-Brown's analysis of it in 1924 (Radcliffe-Brown 1952)—

there is a certain awkwardness about patrilateral cross-cousin marriage that arises at the explanations of both the alliance (structural) and sentiment theorists.

According to Lévi-Strauss's alliance theory, patrilateral cross-cousin marriage is two steps removed from sister-exchange, via uncle-niece marriage: Step 1—Ego gets his sister's daughter for himself as payment for his sister; Step 2—instead of keeping the girl for himself, he gives her to his son.[1] This is a logical progression and not necessarily an historical one (Lévi-Strauss 1969: 446). This type of exchange sets up a short cycle of reciprocity, in contrast to the long cycle set up by the matrilateral form (Lévi-Strauss 1969: 452). Lévi-Strauss finds himself hard-put to explain why any society would choose such an obviously inferior way of forming alliances, between two groups only rather than among many, as is the case with bilateral and matrilateral cross-cousin marriage. His negative attitude toward the patrilateral type is expressed in such pejorative terms as "an abortive form," the "stunted form of so many precocious plants," and so forth (Lévi-Strauss 1969: 448). It could only be a warped mentality that would select the inferior form; and indeed, we see that a preference for patrilateral cross-cousin marriage arises from a "greedy and individualistic attitude" (Lévi-Strauss 1969: 448). It is a cash-and-carry economy of women, deferred, it is true, by a generation, in contrast to direct sister exchange. Analogy becomes reality, and reification leads in wondrous direc-

---

[1] Uncle-niece marriage is of very limited distribution: According to Lévi-Strauss (1969: 432) it is found primarily in parts of South America and among the non-Hindu peoples of southern India. It cannot, therefore, be assumed to be the necessary antecedent of patrilateral cross-cousin marriage everywhere. The best data on this are for the Korava, a Tamil-speaking, low-caste group. According to Thurstone (1909), the uncle has the right to marry his elder sister's daughter or to receive her bride-price. He can keep the girl for himself or marry her to his son. Therefore, it appears that in this case, patrilateral cross-cousin marriage is a by-product of uncle-niece marriage, rather than itself the preferred form. The Korava are strongly Husband Dominant (Thurstone 1909: 442, 448). If patrilateral cross-cousin marriage were the preferred form, that would conflict with the hypothesis presented here. However, that does not appear to be the case.

tions. Yet, how else to explain the choice of the inferior form?

The sentiment theory has its problem too. It proposes that the initial point in the marriage system is Ego the bride-seeker. If he applies to his mother's brother, in the matrilateral form, he is going to a consanguinal kinsman, a man tied by kinship loyalty to his mother and, probably, by affection or duty toward Ego himself. Thus the matrilateral form can be so readily comprehended. However, there is an inherent difficulty in the converse, or patrilateral, form. Ego must either apply to his father's sister, who will be the consanguinal kinswoman, or he must apply to this woman's husband, for their daughter. As to the former, it is unusual for women to have the final right of marriage bestowal over their daughters. There is a hint of this for only one society in this study, Lobi (Labouret 1931: 262), and that is far from clear. If Ego applies to the woman's husband, we leave the sentiment argument altogether. Father's sister might make an agreeable mother-in-law, but her husband has no kin-bound duty or inclination to make Ego a gift of his daughter. The problem here is the point of departure.

Another weakness is the assumption that the choice of spouse is made by the people to be married. In my reading of the ethnographic literature, I have come across very few cases in which choice of partner is solely up to the individual. Even where marriages are not arranged, they must usually be approved by those kin most affected by affinal relationships, exchange of goods and services, and postmarital residence. Therefore, it would seem to make very little difference whether the prospective bride and parent-in-law were the most sentimentally appropriate for the groom.

Toward the end of their book, after analyzing deviant cases, Homans and Schneider (1955) revised their hypothesis. They altered it from a strictly lineal correlation with cross-cousin marriage preference to a correlation between the preferred form of cross-cousin marriage and the locus of authority over male Ego, the bride-seeker. They maintained that Ego turns away from the male who has authority over him, either his father or his mother's brother, and turns to the indulgent male. Therefore, if his father is his authority figure, regardless of the descent system, Ego will be more likely to select his mother's brother as father-in-law; and if his mother's brother is his authority figure, he will select his father's sister for his mother-in-law. This question was brought up when Homans and Schneider discovered three matrilineal societies in their sample that preferred matrilateral cross-cousin marriage. They identified all of these as having jural authority over the boy vested in the father: Kaska and Siriono, correctly, and Garo, incorrectly, as coded for this present study. In their words: "Potestality is a far better predictor than lineality" (Homans and Schneider 1955: 57).

With this point I am in complete accord, and this is, for me, the important finding of their book. However, it does not obviate the criticisms made above. Nor do I agree that it is authority over male Ego that is the important factor here.

In order to test whether authority over children is the most critical factor in the organization of matrilineal domestic groups, I conducted a series of tests on the computer, testing each variable against control over children, whether in the hands of the father or of the mother's brother, or shared. The only variables that correlated with the control variable with $p < .05$ were those variables highly associated with the dominance variable in the initial test. In every case, where presence or absence of the variable was associated with a control pattern, it was associated with a similar dominance pattern; i.e. where a variable was associated with Father Control it was also associated with Husband Dominance, and where it was associated with Mother's Brother Control it was associated with Brother Dominance. The variables showing significant association with control over children are: Bride capture, Woman exchange, Wife's brother disrupts marriage, Brother aggression, Wife's adultery punished by husband, and Husband disposes of wife's sexuality. I found no significant association between control over children and any of the residence patterns, even after rearranging and collapsing data.

Table 1: 10, below, pertains to the problem at hand, whether there is any association between control over children and cross-cousin marriage preference.

It requires no statistical operations to show that there is no significant difference in the distribution of cross-cousin marriage preference between Father Control and Mother's Brother Control. The hypothesis remains that authority over the woman—wife or sister—is the best predictor of the form of cross-cousin marriage preference.

Let us review the argument that leads to this hypothesis. I began with the assumption that in a matrilineal society, the structural core of the kin group is the mother-daughter relationship. (This is not to be confused with Hsu's concept [1965] of the Dominant Dyad: I would not characterize the mother-daughter dyad as the dominant one, in his terms, in most of the matrilineal societies with which I am familiar.) I next assumed that the man who has authority over the mother also has authority over the daughter. By bringing the young man in whom he has a strong personal interest—his son or his sister's son—into the domestic group over which he has control—his sister's or his wife's, respectively—he consolidates his sphere of interest with his sphere of control. In either case, he achieves an at least partial solution to the matrilineal puzzle by uniting, through the marriage of the young pair, his descent group loyalties with his domestic group loyalties.

The weakness of the hypothesis as stated is the assumption that control over minor children follows from control over their mother. While there is a strong association between Husband Dominance and Father Control, and Brother Dominance and Mother's Brother Control, the relationship is not tautological. Each of the control patterns

TABLE 1: 10. Control Over Children and Cross-Cousin Marriage

	Absent	*Matrilateral*	*Patrilateral*
Father Control	16	6	4
Mother's Brother Control	14	5	4
Shared Control	3	4	2

—Father, Mother's Brother, and Shared—is present in at least one case of each of the dominance patterns—Husband, Brother, or Neither. Therefore, although the hypothesized association between dominance pattern and cross-cousin marriage has been confirmed, one of the assumptions underlying it has been shown to be incorrect. How can this be explained?

It appears to be that the man who has authority over the mother has some authority over the daughter, regardless of where ultimate authority over minor children may lie. Apparently this authority is related to the bestowal of the person of the daughter upon the man in whom he has a strong personal interest. To turn the Homans and Schneider hypothesis upon its head, it is the in-law who chooses the groom and not vice versa.

It is also likely that ethnographers, in giving data on control over children, are speaking primarily about boys. It seems that, regardless of who controls the boys, girls are controlled directly by their mothers, so that, indirectly, the ultimate authority over girls resides with the person who controls the mother.

It now becomes necessary to examine the deviant cases, the Brother Dominant societies with preferred matrilateral cross-cousin marriage and the Husband Dominant societies with preferred patrilateral cross-cousin marriage.

DEVIANT CASES

In spite of the statistical significance of the distribution, there is a high proportion of deviant cases, particularly for Brother Dominant societies. Let us examine these.

Brother Dominance with Preferred Matrilateral Cross-Cousin Marriage

There are five cases of this, out of twelve Brother Dominant societies with a stated preference for unilateral cross-cousin marriage. These societies are: Garo, Minangkabau, Mnong Gar, Nayar, and Tsimshian. With the exception of the last, they are all in Asia.

Garo. In this society, the youngest daughter is usually the heiress, inheriting house and land from her mother and, along with it, the obligation to take care of her parents. Marriage is matrilocal. The father will try to find a sister's son to marry his daughter, thus assuring that he will have a subordinate kinsman to look after him in his old age. (If he succeeds, the marriage is avunculocal as well as matrilocal.) While this puts the young husband under the authority of his uncle/father-in-law, and also that of his wife's mother's brother and brother, who are the real heads of the house, it does assure him a secure economic future, more so than if he married a nonheiress and had to set up a new household.

Nayar. Gough's statements on Nayar marriage preference are somewhat confusing: on page 365 she states that, while bilateral cross-cousin marriage is permitted, the matrilateral form is preferred, and on page 366 she posits an increasing preference for patrilateral cross-cousin marriage (Gough 1961a). After some deliberation, I coded "present" for the matrilateral preference.

Nayar marriages can be either with a woman of the same rank or hypergamous, with the man marrying down. The Nayar justify their preference by maintaining that it unites the men of the duolocal household, mother's brother and sister's son, if they have marital interests in the same household, i.e. if the nephew is tied to his wife, the daughter, while the uncle is tied to his wife, the mother (Gough 1961a: 365).

Minangkabau. I was not able to find the details on domestic life that would permit me to explain the "native model" or theory regarding matrilateral preference. The Minangkabau residence pattern, like that of the Nayar, is duolocal, so it is possible that the same explanation is given or understood.

Mnong Gar. Again, details on domestic life are lacking from Condominas's account. However, the preferred spouse is the daughter of the mother's *younger* brother. This implies that there may be a difference in relative rank between families of the marriage system, according to age. This does not, however, mean that the younger brother does not have authority over his older sister. Condominas states: "Baap Can renforça l'influence qu'il exerçait sur sa soeur ainée en exigeant que l'un des fils de celle-ci ... epousat sa fille à lui ... " (Condominas 1957: 30). Residence here is matrilocal, so that in this form of marriage avunculocality would result.

Tsimshian. Unlike their neighbors the Tlingit, the Tsimshian prefer matrilateral cross-cousin marriage. I could find no native explanation on this point. One occurs to me, however. The Tsimshian vested considerable importance in nonmovable goods—houses and insignia posts (so-called totem poles) that were inherited by the sister's son. They also, more than neighboring peoples, allowed women to inherit chiefly names, dancing powers, and initiation into secret societies (Garfield et al. 1951: 28). By marrying the heir to the daughter of the house, it was assured that the privileges vested in the daughter through her clan remained in the house.

For all of these deviant cases it is possible to find a specific explanation. However, just as logical explanations could undoubtedly be given to explain patrilateral cross-cousin marriage if it existed in these societies. What is needed is a general explanation which encompasses or goes beyond the specific theories. That, of course, is the problem of the cross-cultural researcher.

It has been noted by Leach (1951) that matrilateral cross-cousin marriage serves to maintain rank distinctions between intermarrying lineages. This is true regardless of whether the bride givers or the bride takers are superior. Does this explain the deviant cases in the sample?

It obviously could for the Nayar, who have hypergamy built into the marriage system. It possibly could for the Minangkabau and Mnong Gar; I do not have the information necessary to make this decision, nor do I have any information that precludes this possibility. The Garo have no rigid ranking, but it is clearly to the economic and social advantage of the young man to marry into his uncle's household. Whether the bride taker's lineage is inferior to the bride giver's or not, the bride taker himself is certainly subordinate to the bride givers. This explanation gains in plausibility when we consider that these are Asiatic societies, for Lévi-Strauss's (1949) hypothesis of status differential between bride takers and bride givers was empirically based upon Asiatic ethnographic data.

Whether or not this explanation fits the Tsimshian case is another question. The Tsimshian were certainly concerned with rank and status differences, but I have no direct evidence that rank differential was a part of the marriage system. There is a hint, however, that this may have been the case. Although there was no bride-price, marriage being accompanied by gift exchange, the groom's family did provide the greater amount of goods for the exchange. The Tsimshian participated in the Northwest Coast custom of marking rank by the amount of goods given at a gift feast, so that this differential in goods may indicate a differential in rank.

The deviant cases of Brother Dominance with matrilateral cross-cousin marriage preference can be understood as solving the problem of rank differential between intermarrying groups, as Leach (1951) has proposed. This does not conflict with the hypothesis presented here, which posits unilateral cross-cousin marriage as a function of status differential of another kind, that of authority rather than rank. It indicates that in some societies, differences in social rank outweigh in importance differences in domestic authority.

An alternative explanation can be taken from the hypothesis put forward by Eyde and Postal (1961). This is the proposal that matrilocal cross-cousin marriage in matrilineal societies is due to an increase in the unity between men of the lineage within a framework of matrilateral residence. That is, given matrilocal residence, matrilateral cross-cousin marriage results in avunculocality, and the descent tie between mother's brother and sister's son is reinforced by an in-law relationship and common residence.

This explanation suffers from the restriction placed on it of assuming prior matrilocality. While three of the deviant

cases in this sample are matrilocal, two are not. It is, therefore, not as general an explanation as that offered by Leach
(1951). However, the two explanations are not contradictory. As I have proposed in Chapter 8 (p. 82), we can
expect an increase in male cohesiveness within the lineage
as a response to ranking of lineages. One way of emphasizing this cohesiveness in matrilineal societies is avunculocality, where uncle and nephew belong to the same
descent and domestic groups. Another, of course, is duolocality, the residence pattern of the two nonmatrilocal
cases in this deviant case group. Ranked lineages, then,
might be a special case of the larger category of strongly
unified lineages.

Husband Dominance with Preferred
Patrilateral Cross-Cousin Marriage

There are three such cases: Callinago, Lobi, and Santa
Cruz.

Callinago. The Callinago had strong husband authority: the
fully adult man was head of his household, including the
inmarrying husbands of his daughters. (It appears that marriage was matrilocal until a man was able, through some
means not indicated, to establish his own household, of
which he was paterfamilias.) Fathers could even take their
daughters away from their husbands (presumably those residing within their households) and bestow them elsewhere.
The question we must ask is what the advantage would be
to the household head to bring in as husband to his daughter a young man who was in the descent line of neither
himself nor his wife, and whose only tie to him was as the
son of his wife's brother, a man whom he avoids. One
would think that it would be more to his advantage to
bring in his own sister's son. The only suggestion that occurs to me is that this would necessarily create a household
consisting of members of three lineages—male head, female
head and her children, and husbands of daughters—whereas
the matrilateral form would bring together only two. The
patrilateral form thus spreads more widely the network of
necessary and perpetual alliances for each household. As

each extended family household comprised a separate community, this spreading out of community ties may have been advantageous in an area of endemic warfare, for each household would then have three sources of aid—the male head's lineage mates, the female head's lineage mates, and lineage mates of the daughters' husbands.

Lobi. Labouret is confusing on the question of cross-cousin marriage: at one point he says that a man claims a mother's brother's daughter for his own wife or the wife of his son (Labouret 1931: 251), and later (p. 262) he indicates that the brother goes to his sister to ask for her daughter to marry his son. From the context, I considered the latter to be the preferred form, which is patrilateral cross-cousin marriage. This seems to be a variant of the custom among the patrilineal neighbors of the Lobi of the father requesting a newborn girl for his son's future wife. It may be that a man goes to his sister because his sister's husband defers to him and cannot gracefully refuse the request.

Santa Cruz. William Davenport, the ethnographer of Santa Cruz, was kind enough to give me information on patrilateral cross-cousin marriage there. It is preferential in only certain situations, with a total number of such unions less than 5 percent of all marriages. Postmarital residence is virilocal, and girls sometimes marry far away from the lineage locality. In such cases, the women are not able to make use of the garden lands and trees to which they have a claim. When this happens, there will be an attempt to bring back the woman's daughter, via marriage to the mother's brother's son, in the next generation. According to Davenport: "This returns land rights and some continuity from her mother to the mother's natal household" (personal communication, 1972).

How can these exceptions be explained? Patrilateral cross-cousin marriage preferences are limited even in matrilineal societies: of the 25 societies with a preference for unilateral cross-cousin marriage, only 10 choose the patrilateral form. As Robert Lane has pointed out (1962: 496), patrilateral cross-cousin marriage in a matrilineal descent system makes Ego's grandchildren through his son members

of Ego's lineage; however, I do not see how that would explain these deviant cases, as none of them is patrilocal, nor
is there any other indication of a close structural relationship between father and son. It is possible that the data for
the Callinago (taken from historical reconstruction) and the
coding for the Lobi are in error. It may be that there is no
general explanation for these deviant cases, it being likely
that each is deviant for different reasons.

Since I have dealt with a subject which has given rise to
so much acrimony, I feel compelled to insist that preference is not prescription, nor do even the majority of the
actual marriages have to follow the preferred form: the
point here is that the society must be structured so as to
accommodate it. A society may well have several concepts
of what constitutes a "good" marriage, along with the preferred form. Acceptable alternatives are probably necessary
for the marriage system to function at all, unless the marriage classes are so broad as always to provide an acceptable
spouse. Kinship status is only one of the factors contributing to choice of partner, and probably only rarely the most
important one. It is not insignificant that the majority of
societies in the sample, 57.4 percent, do not indicate a
preference for one form of cross-cousin marriage.

If unilateral cross-cousin marriage is so rare, as Homans
and Schneider have indicated (1955: 3), why study it at
all? Their answer, and mine, is that it is a test of theory.
For my study, the confirmation of the hypothesis that unilateral cross-cousin marriage is associated with dominance
pattern supports the concept of the authority pattern as
providing an organizing factor for many facets of domestic
life; its effects can even extend beyond the immediate domestic group and play a part, through marriage preference,
in the formation of the new domestic unit.

We have seen that, for matrilineal societies, unilateral
cross-cousin marriage is one way in which the matrilineal
puzzle is solved, by partially resolving the loyalty conflict
through marriage in the junior generation. But this explanation does not hold for other descent systems, where
there is no such structural puzzle. The broader implications
of the hypothesis, the uniting of persons over whom one

has authority with those in whom one has an interest, however, do hold.

Frazer, who looked upon primitive marriage as an economic exchange, commented that "a father is more anxious to get his niece for nothing for his son than to give his daughter for nothing to his nephew" (cited in Lévi-Strauss 1969b: 439). Yet this contradicts the fact that matrilateral cross-cousin marriage is by far the more prevalent form. Frazer overlooked the fact that Economic Man gives to gain; and by giving a bride, one gains an obligated in-law— one who is, moreover, in the generation that is just coming into its prime. Bride bestowal serves as a link not only between kin groups but also between generations. Where domestic authority patterns are well developed, as they are in the societies coded Husband Dominant and Brother Dominant for this study, bride-bestowal is one way in which a man of the older generation can defer for a while the ceding of authority to the younger generation, by putting a member of that generation in perpetual obligation to him. At least, he can assure for himself an honored place when the inevitable turnover of power occurs. I think it not surprising that unilateral cross-cousin marriage is almost absent from Neither Dominant societies. In these societies, not only is there no concentrated male authority but there is not very much male domestic authority at all. Thus, if one of the functions of cross-cousin marriage is to allow the older generation of men to hold on to some measure of authority and mitigate its loss, it is understandable that there might be little interest in this marriage form in societies in which domestic authority is not an important issue for men.

If the benefits of this marriage form are so obvious, why is it so rare? We can only conclude that, for most societies, factors other than kinship status are perceived as more important in forming alliances. This raises the broader question: under what ecological, demographic,[2] and social conditions is there likely to be unilateral cross-cousin marriage? This question can only be answered by further research.

[2] For a demographic approach, see Ember 1969.

11

Domestic Authority and
the Incest Taboo

The subject of incest has had a long and altogether rather fruitless history in anthropological debate. The question has been very largely one of origins, with no direct evidence to go on, although primatology is now providing us with some indirect evidence concerning the origin of the mother-son taboo. This chapter does not propose to deal with origins, but rather treats the taboo as a social fact, examining its functional relationship to the domestic power structure.

I have defined incest for the purposes of this study as sexual relations between mother and son, father and daughter, and brother and sister. This seems to be the minimal unit within which the restrictions apply universally, or at least to a very wide degree. I do not deal with mother-son incest, as we are concerned here with authority of male over female and the direction of the taboo; sons rarely have authority over their mothers (and then only after they are fully adult and have presumably established sexual relations with females outside the natal home). Furthermore, there is some evidence that the suppression of mother-son sexuality has its roots in subhuman primate social organization (Sade 1968).

The hypothesis stated that the direction of the incest taboo covaries with the pattern of domestic authority. I predicted that in Husband Dominant societies, father-daughter incest will arouse more concern than will sibling incest, and that in Brother Dominant societies, the concern will be with sibling incest more than with father-daughter incest. I expected that in Neither Dominant societies, concern would not be significantly distributed between the two types, and/or both would be considered equally bad. A look at Tables 16: 7 and 17: 7 and the discussions following these tables will show that the hypotheses have been confirmed. In Brother Dominant societies, there is a significant association between the authority of the brother or mother's brother and the especially strong concern over incestuous relations with sister or sister's daughter, a woman over whom male Ego has direct control. In Husband Dominant societies, there is a significant association between the authority of the husband and the especially strong concern over incestuous relations with the woman over whom male Ego has indirect authority—the daughter of his wife—the latter being the woman over whom he has direct authority.

While the hypotheses have been confirmed, one might legitimately ask if authority over the adult woman were the critical variable. Considering that the pattern of authority over the woman and the pattern of control over minor children is significantly associated, with Father Control associated with Husband Dominance and Mother's Brother Control associated with Brother Dominance, is it not possible that it is actually control over children that determines the direction of the incest taboo? To answer this question, I conducted a series of tests. The first test (Table 1: 11) included all of the control patterns and all of the incest attitudes.

TABLE 1: 11. Control Over Children and the Incest Taboo
(Number of cases: 27)

	Sibling Incest Worse	Equal	Father-Daughter Incest Worse
Father Control	5	1	4
Shared Control	1	2	1
Mother's Brother Control	11	1	1

$\chi^2 = 10.52$ $p < .15$

These results were not significant. I then conducted two further tests, one designed to test Father Control and the incest taboo and the other designed to test Mother's Brother Control and the taboo:

TABLE 2: 11.   Father Control and the Incest Taboo

	Father-Daughter Incest Worse	Other
Father Control	4	6
Other	2	15

$\chi^2 = 2.9$ $p < .10$

TABLE 3: 11.   Mother's Brother Control and the Incest Taboo

	Sibling Incest Worse	Other
Mother's Brother Control	11	2
Other	6	8

$\chi^2 = 5.04$ $p < .05$

There is no significant relationship between Father Control and special concern about father-daughter incest, although there appears to be a tendency in that direction. (However, see the reference to Blalock, p. 44.) There is a significant association, though, between Mother's Brother Control and special concern about sibling incest. The pattern of control over minor children, then, is a predictor of the direction of the incest taboo, but the pattern of authority over the adult woman is a better predictor. The brother or mother's brother in a Brother Dominant society is especially enjoined from having sexual relations with the woman over whom he has direct control, his sister and/or sister's daughter; and in Husband Dominant societies, men are most strongly prohibited from having sexual relations with the women over whom they have indirect control, the daughters of their wives. (Obviously, husbands in Husband Dominant societies could not be prohibited from having sexual relations with their wives.) There is, therefore, an association between power over a close kinswoman and an especially strong concern about sexual relations with her. How do we explain this relationship betweeen sex and power?

THE FUNCTIONS OF THE INCEST TABOO

Before we look at possible reasons for the association between the authority patterns and the direction of the incest taboo, it is necessary to consider the functions of this taboo. Although most of the literature on the subject in anthropology deals with the origin of the taboo, the origin is frequently assigned a functional cause; i.e. the taboo is believed to have arisen in response to a social or psychological need of mankind, rather than in response to exigencies placed upon human society by its adaptations to the external environment.

An early theorist in this vein was St. Augustine, who maintained that affinal relationships exist to expand the social sphere of the individual and the group. In *The City of God*, Book XV, Augustine discusses the social poverty of Adam, who was both father and father-in-law to his own children (White 1948). Augustine's theory of incest dwells not so much upon the horror of inmating as upon the social advantages of outmating. The theory entered anthropological thinking via Tylor, and it still holds a respectable position today. As Tylor rephrased the concept (1966: 20) there is the "simple practical alternative between marrying-out and being killed out." It should be noted that St. Augustine and Tylor, like many others to follow, confused incest taboos with exogamy. This is an error, as a prohibition on marriage, which is in almost all societies a formal contract binding two kin groups, is quite a different matter from a prohibition on sexual relations, which need not have this character. All men see sexuality as inevitably linked to marriage, but it was perhaps a bias of our own culture that regarded marriage as coterminous with sexuality. To give just one example to the contrary, the Hopi have no difficulty in differentiating between marriage to a distant clan relative, which is prohibited, and sexual relations with that person, which are not.

The revulsion theory, or the concept that close association leads to revulsion or disinterest between persons of the
opposite sex (Westermarck 1921), was felled by Freudian
researches into the Oedipus complex and related phenom-
ena. It has recently been revived by Wolf, who claims that
his findings on a special form of Chinese marriage corroborate it. This is a marriage between a man and a woman who
had been adopted into his family while a child, as a "sister" and future wife for him. This form of marriage is
usually unhappy (Wolf 1966, 1970). He maintains that
these marital failures are due to revulsion or disinterest
brought about by close association during childhood. To
these findings we could counter the Chinese classic, *The
Dream of the Red Chamber*, in which the hero has no difficulty in responding erotically to women with whom he had
been in the closest contact since infancy, and his deepest
attachment is to a cousin growing up in the same household. As an origin theory, Wolf's theory suffers from the
weakness that these marriages occur in a milieu that already
recognizes the sibling incest taboo, so that the lack of interest between these partners can be plausibly explained as an
extension of the existing taboo into their relationship. In
other words, the sentiment appropriate to a kinsman can be
extended to an outsider who takes over that kinsman's
social role. It is understandable that a man might have difficulty in perceiving a former "sister" as a wife. In terms of
cognitive theory, this would be a situation of cognitive dis-
sonance.

A third functional theory concerns family disruption.
This is based upon the assumption that sexual relations are
potentially disruptive to family life. Both Malinowski
(1931) and Freud (in his many writings on personality development and family experiences) assume that sexuality is
incompatible with domestic tranquility—except, of course,
for the married pair—because uncontrolled sexuality would
lead to competition, jealousy, and hatred. This assumption,
I feel, is founded on a Western bias toward exclusive pos-
session of the sexual object: in many societies, co-wives,
especially if they are sisters, share the same sexual object,

the husband, with apparent amicability. The findings on co-wife jealousy indicate that in 50 percent of the 42 societies for which there were data, jealousy between co-wives who are not sisters is believed to be absent (Table 12: 7). Furthermore, the ethnographic accounts of the domestic life of societies in which sororal polygyny is the norm present a picture of harmony and cooperation between sororal co-wives, even though there may be jealousy in these same societies between co-wives who are not sisters. An example of this is the Crow.

The family disruption theory, however, can be salvaged if we carry it a little further. Sexuality necessarily involves intimacy, and intimacy over time can lead to intensely positive, loving relationships, with almost complete submersion of private wishes into joint concerns, or to intensely negative, or hateful, relationships. Both of these kinds of feelings can be prevented or muted by reducing intimacy, or preserving distance, between individuals.[1] This can go all the way from a recognition of the other's right to privacy, to a respect relationship, to avoidance. The maintenance of the family does not require intense positive bonds and cannot tolerate intense negative ones. By directing sexuality outside the family, the family as a unit can maintain itself. This allows for sex partners, and even spouses, to come and go without disrupting the consanguinal core of the loyalty unit. When the loyalty unit is based upon the marriage re-

---

[1] This theory of the function of the incest taboo has much in common with that proposed by Cohen (1964). Cohen maintains that the incest taboo serves to protect the psychological privacy of the growing child. His thesis is that sexual relations within the family, with persons with whom one already has the strongest of bonds, would create a stimulus overload, beyond the child's capacity to cope. I would counter this argument with two criticisms: (a) this assumes that the incest taboo serves primarily the needs of the child, yet it is instituted, and firmly so, by adults, and (b) while this may have bearing on parent-child incest, it seems to have little bearing on siblings—sexually immature siblings in our own society, and others as well (notably the Goajiro) indulge in sex play without noticeably overstimulating themselves to the point of psychic disturbance. I would agree with Cohen, however, that the incest taboo functions to establish distance between family members.

lationship itself, as it is in Western society, other mechanisms, such as the moral condemnation of divorce, must come into play to buttress it. This hypothesis about the function of the incest taboo is not incompatible with the Augustinian theory, but focuses on the internal structure of the family rather than the family vis-à-vis other family units.[2]

The problem at this point is to explain the variations within the direction of the incest taboo—the reason for the need to suppress certain forms of intimacy more than others. If both father-daughter and brother-sister incest would disrupt the family, why should there be a difference in the strength of the negative attitudes toward them?

We can assume that the greater the likelihood of committing an antisocial act, the stronger the sanctions against it have to be. It follows from this assumption that, other things being equal, incest is more likely, or believed to be more likely, to occur between brother and sister, or mother's brother and sister's daughter than it is between father and daughter in a Brother Dominant society, and between father and daughter than between brother and sister in a Husband Dominant society. If this were not the case, there would be no need for varying degrees of horror or disgust. The question now is, then: What is the relationship between dominance of male over female and overt sexuality?

DOMINANCE AND SEXUALITY

I suggest two alternative hypotheses to explain the covariation of the direction of the incest taboo with the domestic authority pattern. The first holds that a man who

[2] Nor is it an origin theory. The most plausible origin theory with which I am familiar is that put forward by Slater (1959). Her hypothesis is a demographic one, that in the earliest period of human culture, people mated out by necessity due to high infant mortality, short life-span of parents, etc., and this pattern of outmating in early human societies became established and institutionalized as human culture developed. In other words, the response to environmental exigencies created the family as we know it, and once the pattern was set, the incest taboo maintained it even after the exigencies vanished or were lessened.

dominates a woman in other spheres of her domestic life is likely to dominate her sexually as well. In other words, the woman who is dominated is more available to the dominant man as a sexual object than would be other, presumably equally attractive, women. The greater strength of the incest taboo against the dominated female, then, is necessary in order to prevent the dominant male from directing his sexuality toward the available but forbidden female. This relatively simple hypothesis is based upon the assumption that dominance in one sphere overlaps into others, and the strength of the taboo against the dominated female prevents the superordinate male from taking advantage of her accessibility.

The second hypothesis is more complex. It states that the subordinate female is not only more accessible to the dominant male but is more attractive to him as well. Furthermore, her attractiveness does not arise simply from her role as a subordinate object but rather from her seductiveness toward the dominant male. *She* finds *him* the attractive object and is potentially seductive toward him. Thus, the relative strength of the incest taboo serves to protect the susceptible man, not the helpless woman.

There is some ethnographic evidence that this may be the case. I shall give two examples of sibling attraction in Brother Dominant societies. The Trobriand Island myth of sibling incest is one. In this Tristan and Isolde-like tale, careless use of an aphrodisiac causes the brother and sister to fall hopelessly in love. The consummation of their love is followed by tragic death (Malinowski 1953). Another example comes from the Yao. Mitchell states: "The riddle of the initiands—'What is the sweetest fruit which may not be tasted?' Answer, 'Your sister'—neatly reflects the attitude of the Yao" (Mitchell 1956: 146). The problem with using ethnographic data to support this hypothesis is that one can always counter with the argument that incest is secretly desired *because* it is forbidden, and not vice versa.

There are, however, some data on subhuman primate behavior which support the idea that subordinate individuals are attracted to, and seductive toward, dominant ones.

First, there is evidence that social submission may be expressed by means of sexual submission. In at least some species of primates, submission of the subordinate animal, whether male or female, to the dominant male is expressed by presenting, the act of turning to allow the male access to the female's genital area. Among the langurs of North India, presenting, with or without attendant gestures, is the most extreme form of expression of submission short of running away (Jay 1965: 237). For baboons, Hall and Devore state that "presenting is usually done by a subordinate animal, and mounting is usually done by a dominant one" (Hall and Devore 1965: 106). If it were only females presenting only to males, one could infer that female monkeys sometimes use sex as a ploy for diverting attention from the issue at hand or for manipulating the male to their own interest. The fact that this "female" sexual gesture is used by both sexes, however, indicates to me that there is a close tie between sexual submission and general subordination, for the subhuman primates, at least.

Second, we find that subordinate individuals are attracted to dominant ones. Hall and Devore indicate that among baboons, the dominant males receive more positive attention from females than do the subordinate males (Hall and Devore 1965: 106). Schaller reports for the mountain gorilla that females, juveniles, and infants are attracted to the dominant male and seek physical contact with him (Schaller 1965: 346). These are ground-dwelling monkeys and apes, and attraction to the dominant male probably serves as a protective device for the weaker animals, so that they will be close to their defender if danger strikes. Whether or not this pattern is part of the biosocial equipment of the most highly evolved terrestrial primate, homo sapiens, is a moot point.

In offering these suggestions, I am aware of the difficulty in inferring about human cultural responses from primate noncultural ones. There is, however, some evidence from this present study that in human societies, also, subordinate females are attracted to dominant males, and that is the finding that co-wife jealousy is more prevalent in Husband

Dominant domestic groups than in either Brother Dominant
or Neither Dominant ones. Out of 20 Husband Dominant
societies for which there is information, co-wife jealousy is
present in 14, or 70 percent. Out of 10 Neither Dominant
societies for which there is information, this jealousy is present in 3, or 30 percent. The Brother Dominant pattern is
similar to the Neither Dominant one, with co-wife jealousy
present in 4 out of 12 societies, or 33.3 percent (see Table
12: 7). (These findings refer only to co-wives who are not
sisters.)

Co-wife jealousy is often, accounted for by the desire on
the part of the woman to acquire for herself and her children a greater share of the limited goods—material benefits
and other favors—that the husband/father is in a position to
dispense. However, this argument is weak when applied to
matrilineal societies, as in such cases the social and economic status of the woman and her children depend more
upon her lineage than upon her husband. I consider the
most plausible explanation for co-wife jealousy to be that
recognized by most societies themselves, sexual jealousy. By
this I do not mean frequency of sexual intercourse but
rather the position that the wife holds in her husband's
eyes vis-à-vis the co-wives. I am suggesting that sexual jealousy is intensified among women as they feel themselves to
be subordinate to their husbands, as it is upon their attractiveness to the dominant male that their status within the
domestic group depends. This makes the dominant male an
attractive object to them, and any threat to their hold on
him is a threat to their status in the domestic group. As the
husband is not a dominant figure in Brother Dominant or
Neither Dominant domestic groups, there tends to be less
co-wife jealousy. It follows from this that where males are
dominant, females will be seductive; and the more dominant the male, the more seductive will be the behavior of
the subordinate female in order to retain his attraction to
her and the benefits that ensue in the form of status security. What this means for my theory of the direction of the
incest taboo is that the taboo must be especially strong
against sexual relations between the dominant male figure

and the subordinate female, for it is toward the dominant male that the female directs her seductiveness.[3]

We have seen in this chapter that the direction of the incest taboo covaries with the type of domestic authority pattern. While the pattern of control over children does, to a degree, predict the direction of concern about incest, in that there is a significant relationship between mother's brother control and sibling incest concern, a much better predictor is the domestic authority pattern. I have explained this by proposing that in Brother Dominant societies, the brother and/or the mother's brother has direct control over the girl, while in Husband Dominant societies, the father has indirect control over her through his control over her mother. (On this point, see the discussion in Chapter 9, p. 114.) Thus, the degree of concern over type of incest, whether sibling or father-daughter, varies according to who has the greater direct or indirect control over the female object, the sister or the daughter.

We have examined several theories of the functions of the incest taboo. The one I find most compatible with my findings is that incest restrictions enforce distance between family members and prevent the kind of intimacy that can lead either to intense pairing, with the exclusion of interests of others, or to hatred, which would break up the family. Incest taboos are a means by which cross-sex attachments are blocked and prevented from becoming too intense, to the detriment of the family as a unit. Sexual partners, and even spouses, may come and go, but the loyalty unit must remain firm.

Two explanations for the association between the domes-

[3] I believe that this argument could be used to explain the competition and jealousy so often found between mother and daughter in our own society, in contrast to most other societies, where the mother-daughter relationship is one of the most intimate and relaxed of all dyadic relationships. In the western world, the daughter is kept in the natal household, under the authority of the father, long past puberty, without devices such as a respect relationship or avoidance to regulate father-daughter contacts. It can be readily understood, in light of my findings and hypotheses, why the father-daughter incest taboo is so strong in the Western world, while brother-sister incest is regarded, at least in fiction and drama, as a romantic tragedy.

tic power structure and the direction of the incest taboo have been presented. While the first—or more parsimonious —explanation accounts for all the facts as presented in this study, the second is the more interesting, as it extends to the broader realm of primate biosocial behavior and relates to the general question of attraction and jealousy. I have been able to do no more here than allude to some of the tantalizing questions that could be raised if this latter hypothesis were pursued. To do this would require more research, both into primate behavior, to learn more about the biosocial roots of attraction, and in human psychology, to better understand the relationship between the power structure and sexual responses.[4] Attraction can be a strong bonding principle between people, and to dismiss it as the *"je ne sais quoi"* avoids the issue. It merits further study.

---

[4] Erich Fromm has discussed the relationship between the political authority structure and sado-masochism in *Escape From Freedom* (1941), but his thesis is not directly applicable to the issue at hand.

12

Conclusions

A REVIEW OF THIS STUDY

In this discussion on the matrilineal puzzle, I have attempted to show that the critical factor in the puzzle is the allocation of domestic authority over the woman, rather than over children, and that this is handled in essentially three ways: authority of the husband, authority of the brother (or other males of her matriline), and authority of neither. I have, I think, demonstrated that the authority patterns are real syndromes of related traits of both domestic life and broader sociocultural features.

The domestic authority gradient was designed to apply to matrilineal societies, but there is no need to restrict it to those societies. We cannot assume that fraternal authority over adult women is limited in this manner. While it is unlikely that complete Brother Dominance would appear in nonmatrilineal societies, it may well be that varying degrees of brother authority over the domestic group occur in ambilineal, duolineal, or bilateral descent systems. I have already referred to this possibility in certain Japanese communities (see footnote 1 to Chapter 8).

I have shown that there is some association between domestic authority pattern and world area. North America is strongly Neither Dominant. Africa is strongly Husband Dominant. Matrilineal societies in Asia tend to be either Neither Dominant or Brother Dominant, while those in Oceania tend to be either Brother Dominant or Husband

Dominant. An area for future research is an investigation of this distribution.

Therefore, the first of the theorems or major hypotheses, that the model of the domestic authority gradient represents the universe of matrilineal societies, has been confirmed.

The second theorem, that domestic power declines as it disperses, has also been confirmed. To the model of the gradient can be added another dimension, indicating the rise and decline of female autonomy, as illustrated in Figure 6. However, it must be remembered that this pattern is confined to autonomy within the domestic group and does not necessarily indicate high status in the society beyond, as measured by female participation equivalent to male participation in activities that create and perpetuate communitywide ideas and behavior patterns.

FIGURE 6: Domestic Authority and Female Autonomy

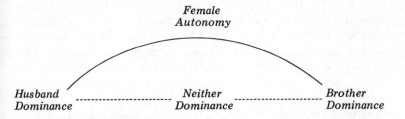

I was gratified that the two hypotheses that I consider to be the most important, those concerning cross-cousin marriage and the direction of the incest taboo, have been supported by the findings. This fact indicates to me that the domestic authority pattern has importance beyond the immediate domestic group, that it feeds into the belief system and the organization of affinal ties.

In the discussion on unilateral cross-cousin marriage, I have demonstrated that the marriage choice can best be predicted by knowing who has authority over the woman to be married and who will, therefore, bestow her upon a man in whom he has a strong interest. In this light, it is easy to explain the small number of societies preferring patrilateral cross-cousin marriage by the small number of societies in which the woman's brother is her domestic authority figure.

It is clear that the different kinds of incest taboos can receive functional explanations beyond a general explanation encompassing the three varieties of the taboo. Furthermore, the findings carry implications about the nature of sexual attraction and lead to a much broader field of investigation.

I must say a few words about the shortcomings of this study. Where it has been least successful, in my opinion, is in indicating the sociocultural factors leading to the three domestic authority patterns, or the inputs. This is particularly true for differentiating between those inputs leading to Husband Dominance on the one hand and those leading to Brother Dominance on the other. The only feature that emerges with clarity here is the differential geographic distribution of the two types, with Husband Dominant societies most prevalent in Africa and South America and Brother Dominant most prevalent in Asia. Both are represented about equally in Oceania and North America. But there is nothing in this study that gives clues as to why the distribution occurs in this manner. This question will require further research.

The second major weakness in this study is that it fails to place the domestic authority pattern within the context of the entire system. This has already been pointed out in Chapter 2. I did not attempt closure of the system, because, at this point, I am only concerned with the authority patterns and their immediate consequences. I shall need inputs more clearly associated with the different patterns before I can theorize how the outputs feed back into the inputs.

BROADER QUESTIONS

In his provocative essay, "Rethinking Anthropology," Leach has called the construction of typologies "arranging butterflies," which "merely reasserts something you already know in a slightly different form" (Leach 1961: 5). This criticism is especially close to the heart of the present study, as one of the examples he used is Richards' (1950) typology of matrilineal social organization. Is Leach being clever, or does his criticism have genuine merit?

First, I feel that it is reasonable to point out that if you know something in a different form, then you know it that way and not as the typology reveals it to you. So, a typology can add to the body of knowledge, if only to point to previously unrecognized relationships and open new lines for thinking and investigation.

Second—and here is the important point—a typology is useful when it can be used for generalizing to a larger scope. What Leach was criticizing, and we must agree with him, is the construction of ad hoc typologies as a means of organizing a limited amount of data, without any consideration of the general nature of their application or their utility beyond the immediate problem. Leach criticized Richards unfairly, for her typology was in the nature of a pilot study and was specifically designed to apply to a restricted body of data; and the utility of her hypothesis about the matrilineal puzzle has been proven by the stimulus it has provided for other works, of which this is only one.

I have asked myself whether Leach's criticism applies to this study. Extending that question, I have asked myself what this study adds to our knowledge about social theory in general and about matrilineal organization in particular.

As for generalizing at the broadest level, I believe that this study has demonstrated and confirmed the importance of the power structure of the domestic group. It should be apparent to the reader by now that domestic authority is not simply another trait, which can be added to or subtracted from a culture without seriously disrupting its organization; rather, the authority pattern serves as the focus for an entire cluster of related traits—or a syndrome if you will—relating to residence, control over property, autonomy of women, and so forth. The factor analyses bear this out and validate the categories. The domestic authority gradient is not an ad hoc typology, applicable to a limited body of data, but rather it applies to the universe of matrilineal societies as represented by this sample.

One of the difficulties of a typology is that it presupposes perfect types, demarcated by boundaries. It is clear that domestic authority syndromes cannot be so pigeonholed—there are too few perfect correlations and too many deviant cases for that. If a refined authority scale were constructed, it is likely that each of the societies in this sample would stand at a different point along it, with greater or lesser degrees of male authority, depending upon some total number of points on the scale. For this reason I prefer to consider the patterns as falling along a gradient rather than into a typology, even though I have had to lump them into crude categories in order to handle the data statistically.

As to the importance of this report for the study of matrilineal kinship, I must accede to Leach's criticism, if it is indeed a criticism, that arranging data "merely" tells us what we already know in another form. I think it quite likely that anyone with any familiarity with the literature realizes that there is considerable variation in the ways matrilineal societies meet the problem of coordinating the descent system with domestic organization: the typologies described in Chapter 1 were constructed for the purpose of analyzing these variations. However, I also believe that for many of us there is the concept of the "true" or "ideal" type of matrilineal society: for the British it may be Ashanti or the Trobriand Islands; for the Dutch, Minangkabau; for the Americans, the Iroquois or the Hopi. By means of the authority gradient, we have seen that the variations are not exceptions to the rule but rather an integral part of the universe of matrilineal kinship. Husband Dominance is as much a reality for matrilineal societies as is Brother Dominance, and women can have high or low degrees of autonomy irrespective of their central position within the descent group.

This leads me to the most damning criticism that Leach makes in the essay cited above, one that all anthropologists with an interest in descent systems must face. He questions whether matrilineality is a real or nominal class. He states:

> In effect Richards's classification turns on the fact a woman's brother and a woman's husband jointly possess rights in the woman's children but that matrilineal systems differ in the way these rights are allocated between the two men. What I object to in this is the prior category assumptions. Men have brothers-in-law in all kinds of society, so why should it be assumed from the start that brothers-in-law in matrilineal societies have special "problems" which are absent in patrilineal or bilateral structures? What has really happened here is that, because Dr. Richards's own special knowledge lay with the Bemba, a matrilineal society, she has decided to restrict her comparative observations to matrilineal systems. Then, having selected a group of societies which have nothing in common except that they are matrilineal, she is naturally led to conclude that matrilineal descent is *the* major factor to which all the other items of cultural behavior which she describes are functionally adjusted [Leach 1961: 4].

If we agree that matrilineality is a nominal rather than a real class, then it hardly merits the attention it has received. As for this present study, that eventuality would not invalidate the authority gradient, but it would certainly undercut its importance as applied to the universe of matrilineal cultures, if that universe were only a nominal construct.

I believe the answer to Leach on this point lies in the study by Aberle (1961), already discussed in Chapter 2. Matrilineal societies emerge as occupying a locus on the societal complexity scale and with a decided geographic distribution, so that if one knew that the kinship system were matrilineal, one would have a better than chance possibility of predicting its placement. This placement strongly implies that matrilineality is adaptive, although the measures used so far are too crude to indicate precisely to what it is adaptive. The most promising suggestions concern residence patterns and labor group organization (Aberle

1961: 726). Aberle's statistical findings impress me as proving the reality of the class "matrilineal societies."

However, Leach's argument reaches further. What he is really asking is: What is a descent system? Is it a fairly arbitrary way of assigning people to one or more groups related by common blood, property, and heritage? Or does the type of descent system of a society condition behavior so that it is different than it would be with another type of descent system? I believe that we can show that descent systems are real in that they have meaning for the way people organize their activities and define their attitudes. Let us explore this on two grounds, structural and cognitive.

A descent group serves many functions. To the members of the group itself, it is probably most important as a loyalty unit. The way the loyalties are parceled out affects the pattern of conflicts and alliances within the community and the society at large. For example, patrilocality with matrilineal descent creates quite a different allocation of sentiment and obligation than does patrilocality with patrilineal descent. Douglas has pointed out that matrilineality as a system tends to disperse loyalties (Douglas 1969: 126), an exception being the rare form of lineage duolocality as practiced by the Nayar and Minangkabau. On a scale of loyalty, from centralized to dispersed, patrilineal descent would be the most concentrated, matrilineal the next, then duolineal—since the kinds of loyalties owed each of the descent groups are usually equivalent although different— and finally bilateral descent as most dispersed.

Not only do descent systems differ in the degree to which they concentrate loyalty but the conflicts engendered by centralized and dispersed loyalties differ also. While it is no doubt true that all descent systems contain built-in conflicts, as Leach implied when he remarked that there are brothers-in-law in all structures, these conflicts are not the same, because the primary kinship loyalties are not structured in the same way. We have had ample demonstration, by Richards and others, of the "matrilineal puzzle." It may be that there is a "patrilineal puzzle" for a woman in a patrilineal society, creating a pull between love and duty to her lineage and her children. I can envision a "bilateral puzzle," pulling the individual between loyalty to the father's side and the mother's, and pitting the parents in an underground battle for the attachment of the child, and so on. The point I am making is that the kinds of loyalty conflicts and alliances, and the effects that these have for broader social organization, are conditioned by the kind of descent system operating in the society, in conjunction with residence patterns and community organization. It is to the descent group that primary loyalties often attach, and other loyalties must not conflict with them irreparably. Whether primary loyalties in fact do or even can always follow the system as required by the culture is a question—failure to do so is the very stuff out of which many of the great dramatic tragedies are made. Primary loyalties are to a large degree structured by the descent system, with consequences for different kinds of conflicts and alliances, and for this reason I feel secure in asserting that descent systems are real and not nominal categories.

I attack Leach on cognitive grounds as well. I propose that the type of descent system conditions people's cognitive sets toward the role of the sexes and the importance of males and females. I was led to this notion by the frequent comments in the ethnographic literature comparing women in matrilineal societies, even male dominant ones, with their patrilineal neighbors. Even where female autonomy is low, my general impression is that it is higher in matrilineal than in patrilineal societies within any given culture cluster. As an example, Loeb compares the better position of Ambo women with the generally low status of women among the neighboring Herero, a patrilineal people (Loeb 1962: 136). It is probable that the importance of the woman as the linking factor in the descent group gives to womanhood a dignity that may be lacking in societies which do not have this belief. In psychological terms, this is saying that in matrilineal societies there is a cognitive set toward the importance of women that has an effect in mitigating male dominance. This is an intriguing theoretical problem, and one that could be investigated further. I hypothesize that the descent system, by emphasizing one parent, both parents equally, or each parent in a different way, conditions the attitude that the individual learns toward sexual differences and carries over in his behavior toward members of the two sexes. If this hypothesis were to be confirmed, it would mean that descent systems are a factor in establishing the individual's image of himself in his sex role and his consequent behavior toward others of the same and opposite sexes. Thus would the reality of the class of descent systems be proven on cognitive as well as structural grounds.

I have saved for this, the concluding, chapter a question that has come up in the literature concerning matrilineal societies, i.e.: Are matrilineal descent systems doomed as these societies meet new challenges and find new possibilities in the modern world? Does the fact that most matrilineal societies exist within the "middle range" of socioeconomic and political development indicate that matrilineality is unsuited to more advanced technology and complex social organization? Gough assumes that it does and she gives an impressive array of examples of the decay of matrilineal descent groups (Gough 1961b). She recounts cases in which the larger descent group recedes as the key kinship unit, while the elementary family emerges. While she does not state that this precipitates the end of reckoning descent through the matriline, the implication is there.

Douglas, on the other hand, analyzes the features of the matrilineal system. She points out that matrilineality has in its favor multiplicity and flexibility of ties between descent groups. She concludes that modern conditions do not necessarily spell the doom of matrilineal systems: on the contrary, matrilineality provides an excellent system for recruitment and organization of property-managing groups under conditions of economic expansion, in "any situation in which competing demands for men are higher than demands for material resources" (Douglas 1969: 130).

A consideration of the domestic authority gradient makes it clear that matrilineality provides for considerable variety and flexibility in domestic organization also. Husband Dominant domestic groups are just as "matrilineal" as Brother Dominant ones; the difference lies in the ways in which the demands and needs of the descent and domestic groups are allocated and met. It is perfectly conceivable for any domestic group type to alter in the direction of any other type without destroying the matrilineality of the descent system.

I should like to mention one case, Minangkabau, that has come to my attention through a discussion with the ethnographer, Nancy Tanner. According to the best-known literature on Minangkabau, which was used for coding this society for the present study, it stands as a clear example of Brother Dominance, with duolocal residence, brother control of property, and the rest. According to Tanner, Minangkabau of today, 50 or 60 years later, is to be coded as Neither Dominant, and the entire emphasis is toward a high degree of female autonomy, with women looking to all close male kin—husbands, brothers, and sons—as resources. Her feeling at the present time is that this pattern may be closer to the precolonial pattern than was the extreme Brother Dominant pattern that existed during the colonial period. That pattern itself may have been a consequence, in part at least, of Dutch colonial policies (Tanner, personal communication, 1970). For Minangkabau, then, it was "modern" conditions that may have led to an intensification of the lineage rather than its dispersal, as Gough would have us believe. In light of this, it becomes somewhat premature to assume that the immediate conditions which seem to indicate a breakdown in lineage solidarity are irreversible and inevitable.

I should like to comment on my own observations of the Hopi in this regard, particularly as Gough uses them as one example of a tendency toward lineage breakdown. She cites Eggan (1950) as a source of information on a tendency toward bilaterality. My fieldwork took place 20 years after Eggan's, and the situation is still much as he described it: among some families, particularly Christians in the "modern" village of New Oraibi, there is a pull toward the

American kinship pattern. However, among the non-Christians, with their religious system centering around clan and lineage roles and responsibilities, the clan system seems as strong as ever. It is true that livestock is handed from father to son, and today fathers and sons are cooperating in the purchase and maintenance of heavy equipment, especially tractors. But these are a man's personal property, not lineage property, and men always had the right to dispose of personal property—including the means to production, such as hoes and bows and arrows—as they pleased. In the traditional sphere of the clan, which includes religious and political rights and duties, the matriline is strong, and women control the home as they did in earlier times.

It may be that the clans will decline in importance. The greatest factor today in producing clan solidarity is the ceremonial system, with rights and duties in it owned by the clans. If and when the ceremonial system breaks down, as seems likely due to the breakdown of native cosmology, the clans may cease to function in any way other than loose exogamous units. They may cease to function at all. However, this does not necessarily mean an end to matrilineality. The matrilineage could persist without the greater clan affiliation. The strength of the matrilineal system in the face of acculturation is evident in the way that the Hopi have adapted English kinship terms, designed for a bilateral system, to matrilineal usage.

In short, I do not fear for the perpetuation of matrilineal descent systems. This is in part because, as Douglas (1969) points out, the descent system itself allows for flexibility. But another important factor contributing to the viability of matrilineal systems is the fact, as can be observed from this study, that the family in matrilineal societies has a variety of possible organizational forms. The domestic group can respond to exigencies brought about by changing environmental conditions without necessarily destroying the descent system, so that matrilineality has every chance of surviving in a modernizing world.

Appendix A: Coding Manual

GENERAL INSTRUCTIONS

Coders are to use a separate code sheet for each ethnographic source. Coding should be done with great exactness: it is better to "overcode" than to "undercode." As far as possible, take every statement in each ethnography at face value—do not try to interpret or read meaning into the statements. To ensure exactness and reduce bias, the coding procedure should be as mechanical as possible.

Each coding decision is to be supported with the quotations from the ethnographic source, including page numbers, upon which the decision to code for that trait was based. Again, "overcode." If the point is made a dozen times, please make sure that each reference is quoted. If it is unclear how a particular point should be coded, make a decision to the best of your ability and indicate on the code sheet that the decision is tentative.

I. CODING FOR TYPOLOGICAL PLACEMENT

A. Statements

The coder is requested to look for any statement by the ethnographer—based either upon his observations or upon native statements—or any quoted statements of natives regarding male authority, or lack of male authority, over the female head of the domestic group. This is asking, for each society: (a) whether any man has authority over the female head (or coheads in polygynous societies in which co-wives are ranked as equals); and (b) if so, which man has the greater authority, the husband of the woman or her brother. It will frequently be found that authority is shared to some degree. In these cases, I ask the coder to estimate in what manner it is shared, whether equally, unequally in favor of the husband, or unequally in favor of the brother.

By authority, I mean legitimate control over the actions of another individual. We understand that in every society, people are constantly exerting influence on the behavior of others. However, our concern here is with relegated authority supported by cultural statements as to how things should be. (This does not mean that many men in husband-dominant societies are not henpecked nor that some husbands do not beat their wives in societies that stress equality and mutual respect—these are deviations from the ideal form and are not relevant to our purposes.)

By female head, I mean the woman who is principally responsible for allocating goods within the domestic group, primarily food. In some cases there are coheads, as when two sisters share a household or when co-wives are equal. In the three-generation household, the female head may be either the younger or the elder adult woman (usually either a mother or a daughter or daughter-in-law).

By husband, I mean the man to whom the woman is married legitimately.

By brother, I mean a male relative belonging to the woman's descent group. This could be a real or classificatory brother, or a real or classificatory mother's brother. For the purposes of the study I am collapsing the statuses "brother" and "mother's brother."

By domestic group, I mean that group of kin, together with occasional additional nonkin (slaves, servants, boarders, etc.), that lives together and cooperates most closely in the production, distribution, and consumption of common property. It serves as a corporate group, in that one or some of its members are authorized to speak for the group as a whole vis-à-vis the society. Its composition may vary widely.

Please code "present," "absent," or "no information" for the following:

1. According to statements by the ethnographer and/or natives, the husband is the authority over the adult woman, her brother having little or no authority over her actions so long as she is married.

2. According to statements by the ethnographer and/or natives, the husband is the primary authority over the woman, but his authority is mitigated by some authority on her brother's part; i.e. the brother has authoritative rights over his sister which put restraints upon the husband's authority. (For example, he may step in to prevent beatings of the sister by her husband, or he may have the right to advise the sister regarding her marriage.)

3. According to statements by the ethnographer and/or natives, neither the husband nor the brother of the female head has more authority than the other. This question is not concerned with the total amount of control exerted over the woman, but rather with who, if anyone, exerts authority within the domestic group. If both do equally, or neither do, code "present" for this trait.

4. According to statements by the ethnographer and/or natives, final control of the woman is vested in her brother, although her husband has limited authority over her. For example, a brother can command a sister to divorce her husband or himself order the husband out. However, the husband would have authority over the wife in certain situations and can legitimately enforce his authority.

5. According to statements by the ethnographer and/or natives, the brother has virtually complete authority over his adult sister, and her husband has little or no control over her actions.

B. Deference Behavior

Deference is the general expression of respect, submissiveness, and obedience. It characterizes unequal relationships. This section is concerned with the question of who defers to whom within the brother-sister/wife-husband triad. Coders are asked to look for two categories of deference behavior, verbal and postural or positional. If either or both kinds are present for any of the relationships listed below, code for "present."

Verbal deference refers to the nonreciprocal use of respect terms; i.e. one of a pair using respect terms to the other, without the other also using respect terms to the first. Frequently, one member of the dyad may address the other only by a term of kinship or other status marker, while the superior may call the inferior by name. Another indication of verbal deference is the use of a separate respect vocabulary on the part of the inferior, which is not reciprocated by the superior. Still another is for the inferior to regulate his tone of voice, usually by softening it. It may also be that the superior is entitled to ask the inferior personal questions which would be considered impertinent to the superior. In order for these restrictions to be considered deference behavior, they must be nonreciprocal. Avoidance behavior—or any other kind of restriction which weighs equally on both members of the dyad—is not to be considered a sign of deference.

Postural or positional deference refers to the nonreciprocal placement of the body. Examples are: the inferior stands while the superior sits; the inferior cannot be positionally higher than the superior; the inferior must nonreciprocally bow, kneel, or crawl; the inferior walks behind, or in front of, the superior, and this is recognized as a sign of deference (and not a practical matter, such as men preceding women on the path in order to defend them); the inferior averts his face while speaking to the superior; the inferior must either cover or bare his head or other parts of his body while speaking to the superior; facilities such as chairs, toilets, doors, etc., are not shared but are differentially used; the two parties do not eat together, or, if they eat concurrently, they sit at different levels or at different places; any other positional or postural indications of relative social rank. Again, these must be nonreciprocal to be considered indications of deference. There may be other indications of deference not covered by the preceding explanations. If so, please code "present" for the appropriate deference relationship and indicate in what manner the deference is exhibited and why, in your opinion, this is a sign of deference.

Please code "present," "absent," or "no information" for the following:

1. Wife defers to husband.

2. Sister defers to brother. (Make certain that this deference is one of sexual status rather than one of age, i.e. junior deferring to senior.)

3. Husband defers to wife's brother or mother's brother.

4. Brother defers to sister's husband.

5. Husband defers to wife.

6. Brother defers to sister.

(Note: It may be that several forms of deference coexist. Be sure that you code carefully for each statement.)

C. Control over Person

In this section, we are concerned with indications, either symbolic or actual, of physical control tolerated by the society of one individual over another. The customs we have chosen to code fall into four categories: marriage rituals, divorce procedures, tolerated aggression, and control of a married woman's minor children.

Marriage rituals. Marriage fulfills a dual function, both uniting two kin groups and establishing a relationship between a man and woman. Since the nature of ritual is, in part, to express social realities, we assume that the marriage rituals will be expressive of the nature of the marital relationship.

One kind of ritual to look for is the ritual of capture. Bride-capture is the most widespread, but groom-capture is also known (among the Garo of Assam, for example). Capture is one of those picturesque customs that few ethnographers overlook if they discuss weddings at all. Therefore, if the ethnographer discusses weddings and does not mention capture, code for "absent." By capture we mean that the captured party makes a real or staged show of resistance to the marriage and is dragged, or otherwise forced, to go through with the marriage by the spouse or his (her) kinsmen. Or, if it is accepted that the bride (or groom) will run away several times and be retrieved by the spouse or his (her) relatives, we can consider this a form of capture. What we are looking for are indications that the spouse is physically torn away from her (his) family. This may of course be staged and the bride, for example, only too eager to join her spouse. What concerns us is the existence of the custom, not whether the bride (groom) actually objects to the marriage.

C1 Code "present," "absent," or "no information" for the following:

1. This society has a ritual of bride-capture.
2. This society has a ritual of groom-capture.

The second kind of marriage ritual we are concerned with is the payment of bridewealth from the groom or his family to the bride's family. (There is also a coding here for groomwealth, although I do not recall ever coming across such a custom.) Bridewealth may be substantial, involving large quantities of subsistence or luxury goods, or it may be primarily symbolic, involving token gifts. We are not to consider any gift by the groom's kin to the couple itself bridewealth, nor, by the same token, is a dowry given by the bride's family to the couple to be considered groomwealth. Among the Tuareg, for example, the groom's family gives the bride's family a gift of livestock, which we classify as bridewealth. The bride's family also gives a substantial gift, but to the couple itself, not to the groom's family; so that we cannot call this true reciprocity. In cases in which each group of kin gives gifts to the other group, e.g. the Hopi, code "absent" for the bridewealth and groomwealth.

Bride service is also to be considered a form of bride-wealth, since the groom gives time and labor instead of, or concomitant with, a payment of goods. The coder is cautioned to be careful here. Cases in which the bride may remain at home for a period before joining her husband, during which her husband visits her, are not to be considered bride service. To qualify as bride service, the husband must be in residence a good part of the time in his bride's family's home and actually perform labor for the woman's kin group.

I ask the coder to estimate whether bride-price is substantial or token. By substantial bridewealth, I mean that a large quantity of goods, relative to the total wealth of the society, changes hands. If the society has a bloodprice, then bridewealth to the amount of or near the amount of the bloodprice for a woman would be considered substantial. In the case of bride service, I have arbitrarily chosen six months or more of continuous labor as substantial. By token bridewealth, I mean that a relatively small quantity of goods changes hands. These will often be goods of a symbolic or luxury nature and will not greatly improve the economic position of the bride's family. A period of continuous bride service for less than six months I consider to be token.

There is one other form of "payment" which I am asking coders to look for, and that is woman exchange. This means that a woman has to be given to the group that provides a man with a wife. It may be a direct exchange made at the time of the marriage, or it may be deferred a generation. The point is that the feeling exists that a woman must replace a woman.

C2 Please code "present," "absent," or "no information" for the following:

1. Substantial bridewealth is exchanged.
2. Token bridewealth is exchanged.

3. Substantial groomwealth is exchanged.

4. Token groomwealth is exchanged.

5. Substantial bride service is paid.

6. Token bride service is paid.

7. Woman exchange is practiced.

(Note: We are concerned only with first marriages for the woman, and with marriage with a woman of equal rank to the husband.)

Divorce procedures. Our concern is with who casts out whom. In some societies, such as our own middle class, divorce is ideally a joint decision, arrived at rationally and conducted in a "civilized" manner. In other societies, one party or the other, or even a third party, is regarded as the disrupter of the marriage, regardless of the true facts in any individual case.

Coders are requested to assess whether the wife leaves—in which case she bears the brunt of the disruption—or whether the husband leaves—in which case the reverse is true. Finally, in some matrilineal societies the wife's brother or mother's brother formally initiates the divorce by asking or commanding the husband to leave or commanding the sister to dismiss her husband.

C3 Code "present," "absent," or "no information" for the following:

1. The husband casts out the wife, or she leaves.

2. The wife casts out the husband, or he leaves.

3. The wife's brother or mother's brother disrupts the marriage.

4. Another form of disruption takes place. (If coded "present," please specify.)

C4 Tolerated aggression. Because of the nature of marriage, which demands intimacy and the acting out of impulses, it is likely that a certain amount of aggression of husbands toward wives, and vice versa, is tolerated in most societies. (By this I mean the occasional slap, throwing of dishes, and the like.) But not all societies allow husbands to kill, maim, or publicly humiliate their wives. I ask coders to determine whether severe aggression on the part of the husband against the wife is tolerated.

By severe, I mean any beating that goes beyond a light cuffing; cutting or burning; public humiliation, such as holding up the wife to mockery or allowing one's friends or relatives to beat or rape her.

By tolerated, I mean behavior which is approved or against which there are no sanctions beyond gossip or general dislike. If the wife's kinsmen, or other members of the society, are legally entitled and morally obligated to take action against a husband who injures the wife, then this behavior is not considered to be tolerated.

The brother-sister relationship is of a different nature. In almost all societies, incest taboos enforce a degree of social distance and repression of impulses. Therefore, we do not expect severe physical aggression to be common. What we are concerned with here, rather, is whether or not a brother can in any way threaten or punish an adult sister.

By threaten, I mean that he can call down natural or supernatural sanctions against a sister who thwarts him, to a greater degree than could any member of the society threaten any other member.

By punish, I mean that the adult brother has the power to withhold necessary goods and services from his married sister, or that he can actually punish her corporally or directly cause others to do so.

Code "present," "absent," or "no information" for the following:

1. Severe aggression against the wife by the husband is tolerated.

2. Brothers are entitled to threaten or punish their adult, married sisters.

C5 Control of minor children. Coders are asked to assess the ultimate control over minor children who live with their mother. If the husband and wife coreside, then the day-to-day instructions and punishments for minor infractions will be likely to fall to both parents. In many societies, it is the father who pays or receives damages and has the power to punish severely, or even kill. In others, it is the mother's brother. In still others, father and mother's brother may share responsibility more or less equally, or each may be responsible for different kinds of severe infractions. If the mother's brother has the right to sell into slavery, or to pawn, or to demand for a member of his household, or otherwise to make major decisions about the child of a married sister, this is to be considered control by the mother's brother. If the father has these rights, or if the mother's brother must ask the father's permission, then the father is to be considered as having ultimate control. If neither male has legal control (e.g. if ultimate control of minor children is vested in the mother), then code "absent" for both statements. If father and mother's brother share control more or less equally, so that it is impossible to determine which has greater control, code "present" for both statements.

Code "present," "absent," or "no information" for the following:

1. Ultimate control over minor children is the responsibility of the father.

2. Ultimate control over minor children is the responsibility of the mother's brother.

D. Control over Property

In this section, we are concerned with the individual who exerts the greatest control over the common goods of the domestic group, whatever the composition of that group may be.

Common goods refers to anything that is owned and/or used jointly by members of the domestic group, or that is collectively produced by them. By extension, it also refers to time and energy (i.e. labor) used in productive activities for the benefit of the group. Goods can be either material (such as tools, heirlooms, cash, food supply, etc.) or non-material (such as titles, the right to hold certain positions in the society, etc.).

By control, I am referring to the recognized right to dispose of, allocate, or withhold common goods without the formal consent of other adult members of the domestic group. I also refer to the right to allocate the time and labor of productive members. This latter kind of control may not be specified for all societies.

Coders are asked to assess the relative degree of control over domestic group goods by husband, wife, and wife's brother. If the husband organizes the labor of the household, receives and distributes what is produced, and has ultimate authority over the utilization of domestic group resources, then we must consider that he has almost total control. If other members of the group, such as the wife, have control over part of the common goods (e.g. they own part of the family herd), which they can utilize or dispose of without asking permission, but if control over most goods and labor is vested in the husband, then he is to be considered as controlling a major portion. If the material objects of the household belong primarily to the wife, or if she organizes the labor of the household, then she can be considered in control. In some cases, the adult married woman's brother allocates almost all goods and duties, and thus he would be in control. (This is likely to be true only in cases of matrilocal or duolocal residence.) Finally, we have a statement regarding partial control by the brother. In this case, the wife's brother receives a considerable portion of the goods of the domestic group without giving an equivalent return, although he may give token gifts. His portion is a gift, but not a free gift: it is a gift to which he has a clearly defined right. Therefore, it is appropriate to assume that the brother has some control over the property of the domestic group, since he is entitled to a portion of it.

Code "present," "absent," or "no information" for the following:

1. The husband controls almost all domestic group property.

2. The husband controls a major portion of domestic group property.

3. The wife controls the major portion of domestic group property.

4. The brother controls a significant portion of domestic group property.

5. The brother controls almost all domestic group property.

6. The sister controls almost all domestic group property (of which her brother is male head).

II. CODING FOR TRAITS

The traits we are concerned with in this part of the coding are those having to do with relationships within the family and the status of women in and out of the home.

A. Degree of Female Autonomy

In this section I am concerned with the freedom of women to determine decisions, control activities of the domestic group, and participate in community affairs. The coder is asked to look for indications of plural marriage, sexual restrictions, and the right to hold important social positions.

A1 Plural marriage. By plural marriage I mean the right to have more than one spouse at a time. Polygyny means plural wives; polyandry means plural husbands. Sororal polygyny refers to a preference for marrying women who are sisters.

Code "present," "absent," or "no information" for the following:

1. Polygyny is allowed but limited (under 20%).

2. Polygyny is allowed and general (20% and over).

3. Sororal polygyny is the preferred form.

4. Nonsororal polygyny is the preferred form.

5. Co-wives (who are not sisters) are believed to be jealous of one another.

6. Polyandry is allowed.

A2 Sexual restrictions. In many societies, sexual restrictions weigh more heavily upon the wife than on the husband, and punishment for infractions is harsher. The statements below are to be taken as referring to most of the people most of the time. There may be special social roles, such as that of the sister of the king, in which the woman is allowed greater than normal sexual freedom. Also, there may be periods of sexual license, such as harvest festivals, during which the usual restrictions do not apply. We are not concerned with these exceptions, but with the usual behavior for most wives. If there is different behavior required for different kinds of wives, code for the first wife and/or the wife having social status closest to the husband; i.e. in such cases disregard behavior required of concubines or slave wives.

Adultery refers to sexual relations with anyone who is not a socially recognized sex partner. Legitimate sex partners always include the spouse. They may also include certain categories of consanguinal or affinal kin. By "allowed," I mean that sexual relations with persons outside the socially recognized sex partner category are generally overlooked by the society, or even condoned. By "disposing of wife's sexuality," I mean that a husband can give or lend his wife to another man for sexual purposes. By "without her consent," I mean that he can force her to do this or punish her if she refuses.

Code "present," "absent," or "no information" for the following:

1. Adultery is allowed for husbands.

2. Adultery is allowed for wives.

3. Wife's adultery is punished by the husband or his kin group.

4. Wife's adultery is punished by her brother or her kin group.

5. Husband can dispose of wife's sexuality without her consent.

A3 Social positions. In this section, the coder is asked to determine what opportunities there are in the society for women to hold positions of social significance outside the home. These are to be positions of importance in their own right, not simply status positions held by virtue of being someone's mother, sister, wife, or daughter.

By "ascribed," I mean inherited or married into. By "achieved," I mean acquired through one's own efforts.

Code "present," "absent," or "no information" for the following:

1. Some women hold ascribed political or religious positions, which cannot be held by men.

2. Some women hold achieved political or religious positions, which cannot be held by men.

3. Some women hold ascribed political or religious positions, which can also be held by men.

4. Some women hold achieved political or religious positions, which can also be held by men.

5. Women hold public rituals; that is, they perform in front of men (and other women and children).

A4 Menstrual restrictions (adapted from Stephens 1963: 404). The purpose of this coding is to assess the severity of restrictions placed upon menstruating women and the reasons given for these restrictions. Our concern is not necessarily with first menstruation but with all menstrual periods. I have divided the severity of restrictions into four levels, from most to least severe.

By seclusion, I mean that the woman is removed from contact with men. This usually requires a menstrual hut or room. By "esthetic reasons," I refer to feelings of dirtiness, messiness, likelihood of staining the bedding, unspecified embarrassment.

Code "present," "absent," or "no information" for the following:

1. The menstruating woman is secluded from men.

2. The menstruating woman must not be involved in preparing food that will be eaten by men.

3. Other restrictions are placed upon the menstruating woman's behavior (beyond a taboo on sexual relations).

4. There exists the feeling that a man should not have intercourse with a menstruating woman.

5. If (4) is present, this is for esthetic reasons.

6. If (4) is present, this is to protect the man from harm.

7. Menstrual restrictions are said to protect the woman.

8. Menstrual restrictions are said to protect objects and/or people against possible dangers caused by the menstruating woman.

9. If (8), menstrual blood or the presence of a menstruating woman has a harmful effect upon ritual objects.

10. If (8), menstrual blood or the presence of a menstruating woman has a harmful effect upon the food supply (either wild or domesticated plants or animals).

11. If (8), menstrual blood directly harms men who come into contact with it.

B. Preferential Marriage

In this section we are concerned with the preferred form of first marriage. The point of reference is male. The type of cousin may be either real (if the parents of the cousins are true siblings) or classificatory (when the parents of the cousins are not true siblings but use sibling terms to one another).

Code "present," "absent," or "no information" for the following:

1. Marriage with matrilateral parallel cousin (mother's sister's daughter) is preferred.

2. Marriage with partilateral parallel cousin (father's brother's daughter) is preferred.

3. Marriage with matrilateral cross cousin (mother's brother's daughter) is preferred.

4. Marriage with patrilateral cross cousin (father's sister's daughter) is preferred.

(Note: If several forms are allowed, try to assess which, if any, is preferred. If there is no true preference, code "present" for the allowed forms.)

If the answer to all of the above is "no" or "no information," code for the following:

5. Marriage is preferred with a female linked to Ego through his mother, but not the child of her real or classificatory sibling.

6. Marriage is preferred with a female linked to Ego through his father, but not the child of his real or classificatory sibling.

C. Sibling Incest

Unless otherwise specified, siblings referred to are siblings having at least the mother in common. Incest refers to sexual relations of any kind after puberty.

Code "present," "absent," or "no information" for the following:

1. Sibling incest is regarded as worse than father-daughter incest.

2. Sibling incest is equal to father-daughter incest in the degree of horror, repulsion, or amusement with which it is regarded.

3. Sibling incest is regarded as less antisocial than father-daughter incest.

4. Sibling incest is considered extremely bad and results in severe social or supernatural punishment to the offenders and/or their kin group.

5. Sibling incest is regarded as scandalous but punishment is fairly mild, e.g. payment of a fine, enactment of a ritual of purification, etc.

6. Sibling incest is regarded as bad, but no immediate social or supernatural sanctions are applied.

7. Sibling incest is prohibited, but violations are not severely regarded, i.e. they may cause amusement or a reaction of indifference.

8. Sibling incest is permitted, at least to some members of the society under some conditions, the most common form being sibling marriage.

9. Marriage is permitted between classificatory siblings (specify which).

10. Marriage is prohibited, but sexual relations are permitted, between classificatory siblings (specify which).

(Note: The ethnographer may not give a direct statement about incest. If this is the case, examine myths and tales for indications of incest and reactions to it.)

D. Avoidance

Coders are asked to assess whether, and to what degree, adult cross-sex siblings or fathers and daughters tend to avoid one another. By "avoidance" I mean either a rule that they are not to directly look at, speak to, or even be in the same room with one another (except perhaps in life-or-death emergencies), which will be considered total avoidance, or a rule or feeling that there should be little contact between them and that only of the most formal kind and under conditions of necessity. This shall be considered partial avoidance.

Please code "present," "absent," or "no information" for the following:

1. Adult brothers and sisters totally avoid one another.

2. Adult brothers and sisters partially avoid one another.

3. Adult daughters and their fathers totally avoid one another.

4. Adult daughters and their fathers partially avoid one another.

Appendix B: Coding Bibliography[1]

Ambo (2d quarter, 20th C.) I. A: 75-76, 79, 109, 134, 257. B: 136. C1: 248. C2: 252. C3: 257. C4: 59, 134. C5: 225. D: 109, 152. II. A1: 106, 133, 136. A2: 75-76, 136, 137. A3: 42, 122. A4: 76, 250. B: 103. C: 18, 317. D: 106.

Loeb, Edwin M., 1962, "In feudal Africa," *IJAL 28, no. 3, part 2.*

Ashanti (late 19th C.—early 20th C.) I. A: (a)7. B: (b)65, 69. C1 and C2: (a)24. C3: (a)20, 22; (b)70. C5: (a)8-10, 17, 18. D: (a)4, 336. II. A1: (a)27. A2: (b)58. A3: (c)83, 158. A4: (c)81, 82, 96, 131. B: (a)19. C: (a)304. D: (a)19; (b)69.

(a) Rattray, Robert Sutherland, 1929, *Ashanti law and constitution*, Oxford, Clarendon Press.

(b) Lystad, Robert A., 1958, *The Ashanti; a proud people*, New Brunswick, Rutgers University Press.

(c) Rattray, Robert Sutherland, 1923, *Ashanti*, Oxford, Clarendon Press.

---

[1] Where no page reference is given, there is no information, with the exception of IC3: 1 and 2, which are derived from the residence rules. Abbreviations: *AA—American Anthropologist*; BAE—Bureau of American Ethnology; HRAF—Human Relations Area Files; *IJAL—International Journal of American Linguistics*; *JRAI—Journal of the Royal Anthropological Institution of Great Britain and Ireland*; *SWJA—Southwestern Journal of Anthropology*; WES—"World Ethnographic Sample."

Aua (1st quarter, 20th C.) I. A: 430, 432. C1 and C2: 432. C3: 433. C5: 432. D: 432. II. A1: 433. A3: 430. B: 433.

Pitt-Rivers, G. L. F., 1925, "Aua Island: ethnographical and sociological features of a South Sea pagan society," *JRAI 55:* 425-38.

Belu (2d quarter, 20th C.) I. A: 410, 423. B: 425. C1 and C2: 287. C3: 388-89. C4: 413. C5: 423. D: 410, 411, 414, 416. II. A1: 375, 378. A2: 379-80. A3: 559, 569, 173-74. A4: 430. B: 267-68. C: 263. D: 442.

Vroklage, B. A. G., 1952, *Ethnographie der Belu in Zentral-Timor*, Leiden, E. J. Brill.

Bemba (2d quarter, 20th C.) I. A: (a)115, 174; (b)32, 159. B: (a)103, 107, 135, 126, 191; (b)50, 81. C1 and C2: (a)113. C3: (a)143. C4: (a)174, 191. C5: (a)111. 115, 143; (b)159. D: (a)102, 190, 191, 193. II. A1: (a)110, 129; WES. A2: (b)50, 71. A3: (a)24; (b)38. A4: (b)31-32. B: (b)106. C: (a)190; (b)34. D: (a)115, 140, 191.

(a) Richards, Audrey I., 1939, *Land, labour and diet in Northern Rhodesia: an economic study of the Bemba tribe*, Oxford, published for the International Institute of African Languages and Cultures by the Oxford University Press.

(b) Richards, Audrey I., 1956, *Chisungu: a girls' initiation ceremony among the Bemba of Northern Rhodesia*, London, Faber and Faber.

Bororo (ca. 1936) I. A: (a)272. B: (a)287. C3: (a)272. D: (a)277, 278. II. A1: (a)276; (b)430; WES. A4: (b)422. B: (a)282.

(a) Lévi-Strauss, Claude, 1936, "Contribution à l'étude de l'organisation sociale des Indiens Bororo," *Société des Américanistes, Journal, n.s. 28:* 269-304.

(b) Lowie, Robert H., 1948, "The Bororo," *U.S. BAE, Bulletin 143, vol. 1:* 419-34 (secondary source).

Callinago (17th C.) I. A: (a)13; (c)182-83. B: (a)12, 13; (c)182. C1 and C2: (e)558. C3: (b)25. C4: (b)25. C5: (e)550. II. A1: (b)24, 25. A2: (e)556. A3: (a)5, 7; (e)561. A4: (b)25. B: (c)188; (d)289. C: (c)188. D: (c)188.

(a) Breton, Raymond, and Armand de la Paix, *An account of the Island of Guadeloupe* (HRAF translation from *Histoire Coloniale 1:* 45-74, Paris, 1929).

(b) Breton, Raymond, ca. 1930, "Observations of the Island Carib: a compilation of ethnographic notes" (HRAF 1958).

(c) Taylor, Douglas Macrae, 1946, "Kinship and social structure of the Island Carib," *SWJA 2:* 180-212.

(d) Taylor, Douglas Macrae, 1957, "Marriage, affinity, and descent in two Arawakan tribes: a sociolinguistic note," *IJAL 23:* 284-90.

(e) Rouse, Irving, 1948, "The Carib," *U.S. BAE, Bulletin 143, vol. 4:* 547-65.

Cochiti (ca. 1922) I. A: (b)368, 369. B: (a)82. C1 and C2: (a)84. C3: (a)31. C4: (a)31. C5: (a)32-33. D: (a)27, 28. II. A1: (a)84. A2: (a)31. A3: (b)368-69. A4: (a)83. B: (a)15. D: (a)82.

(a) Goldfrank, Esther, 1927, "The social and ceremonial organization of Cochiti," *American Anthropological Association Memoirs 33.*

(b) Lange, Charles H., 1959, *Cochiti*, Austin, University of Texas Press.

Coniagui (ca. 1950) I. A: 41. B: 51-52. C1 and C2: 65. C4: 66. C5: 41. D: 23, 28, 29, 66. II. A1: 23. A2: 66. A3: 72.

Lestrange, Monique de, 1955, *Les Coniagui et les Bassari*, Paris, Presses Universitaires de France.

Creek (ca. 1912) I. A: (a)81. B: (a)368, 385. C1 and C2: (a)369; (b)117. C3: (a)353. C4: (a)346-52, 354. C5: (a)114, 365. D: (a)79, 336, 337. II. A1: (a)79, 370. A2:

(a)346-52, 353. A3: (a)100, 164, 367. A4: (a)356-59. B: (a)166. C: (a)355. D: (c)705.

(a) Swanton, John R., 1924/1925, "Social organization and social usages of the Indians of the Creek Confederacy," *U.S. BAE, Annual Report 42:* 23-472, 859-900.

(b) Speck, Frank G., 1907, "The Creek Indians of Taskigi Town," *American Anthropological Association, Memoir 2:* 99-164.

(c) Swanton, John R., 1946, "The Indians of the Southeastern United States," *U.S. BAE, Bulletin 137.*

Crow (ca. 1880) I. A: 57, 101, 188. B: 26, 29, 259-60. C1 and C2: 50. C3: 53. C4: 26, 60. C5: 50, 54, 57. D: 13, 53. II. A1: 50, 51, 60. A2: 19, 22, 47, 48, 55, 101, 188. A3: 47, 60, 61, 281-82. A4: 44, 45. B: 45, 46. C: 43, 44, 45. D: 26, 30.

Lowie, Robert Harry, 1935, *The Crow Indians*, New York, Farrar and Rinehart.

Darfur (late 19th C.—early 20th C.) I. A: (a)224. B: (a) 210, 217; (b)10, 11. C1 and C2: (a)227; (b)20. C3: (b)12. C4: (a)232. C5: (b)15, 19, 34. D: (b)10, 22, 34. II. A1: (a)234, 235; (b)20. A2: (a)232, 233; (b)21. A3: (c)63, 64, 93. B: (b)18; (c)60. D: (c)106-07.

(a) Felkin, Robert W., 1885, "Notes on the For tribe of Central Africa," *Royal Society of Edinburgh, Proceedings 13:* 205-65.

(b) Beaton, A. C., 1943, "The Fur," *Sudan Notes and Records 29:* 1-39.

(c) MacMichael, Harold A., 1922, *A history of the Arabs in the Sudan, vol. 1*, Cambridge, University Press.

Delaware (early 18th C.) I. A: (a)38, 49; (c)9. C1 and C2: (a)37. C3: (c)8. C5: (a)34. D: (a)21. II. A1: (a)38; (e)81; WES. A2: (a)38, 39. A3: (c)13, 14; (b)220; (a)49, 52. A4: (a)36; (b)215. B: (a)45. D: (d)33-34.

(a) Newcomb, William W., Jr., 1956, "The culture and acculturation of the Delaware Indians," *Michigan, University, Museum of Anthropology, Anthropological Papers 10.*

(b) Harrington, Mark R., 1913, "A preliminary sketch of Lenape culture," *AA, n.s. 15:* 208-35.

(c) Wallace, Anthony F. C., 1947, "Woman, land, and society: three aspects of aboriginal Delaware life," *Pennsylvania Archaeologist 17:* 1-35.

(d) Wallace, Anthony F. C., 1950, "Some psychological characteristics of the Delaware Indians during the 17th and 18th centuries," *Pennsylvania Archaeologist 20:* 33-39.

(e) Zeisberger, David, 1910, *David Zeisberger's history of the northern American Indians,* edited by Archer Butler Hulbert and William Nathaniel Schwarze, Columbus, Fred J. Heer.

Dieri (late 19th C.) I. A: (a)41. B: (b)72; (c)194. C1: (a)61. C2: (a)41; (b)72. C4: (a)59, 61. C5: (a)59. II. A1: (a)53; (b)76; (c)194. A2: (a)41. A3: (c)198, 201. A4: (c)194, 195. B: (b)58, 59, 70. C: (a)47, 70. D: (b)70, 71.

(a) Howitt, Alfred W., 1890, "The Dieri and other kindred tribes of Central Australia," *JRAI 20:* 30-104.

(b) Elkin, Adolphus P., 1938, "Kinship in South Australia," *Oceania 9:* 41-78.

(c) Berndt, Ronald M., 1953, "A day in the life of a Dieri man before alien contact," *Anthropos 48:* 171-201.

Garo (ca. 1955) I. A: (a)81-82, 92, 168. B: (a)81-82, 92, 124; (b)77. C1: (a)83, 85. C2: (a)83, 85. C3: (a)169, 170. C4: (a)258; (b)75. C5: (a)112-14, 132. D: (a)74, 131. II. A1: (a)148, 149. A2: (a)74, 113. A3: (a)66, 167. A4: (a)98. B: (a)80. D: (a)172.

(a) Burling, Robbins, 1963, *Rengsanggri: family and*

kinship in a Garo village, Philadelphia, University of Pennsylvania Press.

(b) Nakane, Chie, 1967, *Garo and Khasi: a comparative study in matrilineal systems*, Paris and The Hague, Mouton.

Goajiro (1st quarter, 20th C.) I. A: (a)95, 96. B: (a)104; (e)9-10. C1 and C2: (a)31. C3: (a)95. C4: (a)100. C5: (a)31-32, 63. D: (a)94, 95, 104. II. A1: (a)82, 107. A2: (d)380. A3: (a)129, 182-83; (d)380. A4: (a)138. B: (c)60. C: (b)45, 69, 94. D: (b)69; (c)60; (e)5-6, 10.

(a) Bolinder, Gustaf, 1957, *Indians on horseback*, London, Dennis Dobson.

(b) Gutierrez de Pineda, Virginia, 1948, "Organización social en la Guajira," *Bogotá, Instituto Etnológico Nacional, Revista 3, no. 2* (HRAF translation).

(c) Wilbert, Johannes, 1950, "Kinship and social organization of the Yekuana and Goajiro," *SWJA 14:* 51-60.

(d) Armstrong, John M., and Alfred Métraux, 1948, "The Goajiro" *U.S. BAE, Bulletin 143, vol. 4:* 369-83.

(e) Santa Cruz, Antonio, 1941, "Aspects of the avunculate in the Guajiro culture," *Primitive Man 14:* 1-13.

Guanche (ca. 1500) I. A: (a)35. C1 and C2: (a)35. C3: (a)35. C5: (a)36-37; (b)479. II. A1: (b)478. A2: (b)480. A3: (b)487. B: (a)35. C: (a)35, 37. D: (a)37.

(a) Espinosa, Alonso de, 1907 (written 1580-90), *The Guanche of Tenerife*, C. M. Markham, ed. and trans., London, Hakluyt Society.

(b) Cook, Alice Carter, 1900, "The aborigines of the Canary Islands," *AA, n.s. 2:* 451-93 (secondary source).

Gure (ca. 1930) I. A: (a)193; (b)50. C1 and C2: (a)192. C3: (a)193. C5: (a)189. II. A1: (b)52; WES. A2: (b)52. B: (a)190, 191; (b)51-52.

(a) Meek, Charles K., 1931, "The Gure," in his *Tribal*

Studies in Northern Nigeria, vol. 2, London, Kegan Paul, Trench, Trübner: 189-203.

(b) Gunn, Harold D., 1956, *Pagan peoples of the central area of northern Nigeria*, London, International African Institute.

Hopi (ca 1965) Coded by ethnographer, Alice Schlegel.

Iroquois (1st half, 19th C.) I. A: (b)65; (c)171. B: (b)99, 122. C1 and C2: (a)322. C3: (b)66. C4: (g)32. C5: (a)325. D: (a)326. II. A1: (a)324. A2: (a)331; (g)31. A3: (c)172; (d)469; (e)268. A4: (f)301. D: (c)179; no mention in any source.

(a) Morgan, Lewis H., 1962, *League of the Ho-de-no-sau-nee or Iroquois*, New York, Citadel Press (first published 1851).

(b) Morgan, Lewis H., 1881, "Houses and house life of the American aborigines," *U. S. Geographical and Geological Survey of the Rocky Mountain Region, Contributions to North American Ethnology 4.*

(c) Randle, Martha C., 1951, "Iroquois women, then and now," *U.S. BAE, Bulletin 149:* 167-87.

(d) Goldenweiser, Alexander A., 1912, "On Iroquois work," *Canada, Geological Survey, Summary Report 1912:* 464-75.

(e) Quain, Buell H., 1937, "The Iroquois," in Margaret Mead, ed., *Cooperation and Competition among Primitive Peoples*, New York, McGraw-Hill: 240-81 (secondary source).

(f) Murdock, George P., 1934, "The Iroquois of northern New York," in his *Our Primitive Contemporaries*, New York, Macmillan: 291-323 (secondary source).

(g) Parker, Arthur C., 1913, "The code of Handsome Lake, the Seneca prophet," *New York State Museum, Bulletin 163.*

Kaska (early 20th C.) I. A: (a)124, 126; (b) 134. B: (a)126, 130; (b)77. C1 and C2: (a)192. C3: (a)142. C4: (a)163; (b)91-92. C5: (a)129, 182. D: (a)142, 143. II. A1: (b)129, 132, 133. A2: (a)126, 163, 164. A3: (a)173-74; (b)107. A4: (b)123-24. B: (a)129; (b)131. C: (a)150, 164; (b)91. D: (a)189; (b) 77.

(a) Honigmann, John J., 1949, "Culture and ethos of Kaska society," *Yale University Publications in Anthropology 40.*

(b) Honigmann, John J., 1954, "The Kaska Indians: an ethnographic reconstruction," *Yale University Publications in Anthropology 51.*

Khasi (early 20th C.) I. A: (a)78-79; (b) 125, 130. B: (a)82. C1 and C2: (a)127-28; (b)124. C3: (a)80; (b)130. C4: (a)93. C5: (b)124, 125. D: (a)82, 83; (b)103, 131. II. A1: (b)137. A2: (a) 80, 93; (b)137, 139. A3: (a)70. B: (a)78; (b)118. C: (b)119; (c)129. D: (b)125, 130; (d)210.

(a) Gurdon, Philip R. T., 1907, *The Khasis*, London, David Nutt (2d ed., 1914, London, Macmillan).

(b) Nakane, Chie, 1967, *Garo and Khasi: a comparative study in matrilineal systems*, Paris and The Hague, Mouton.

(c) Roy, David, 1938, "The place of the Khasi in the world," *Man in India 18:* 122-34.

(d) Mukherjee, Bhabananda, 1958, "Social groupings among the Khasis of Assam," *Man in India 38:* 208-12.

Kunama (ca. 1850) I. A: 489. C1 and C2: 487. C3: 489. C5: 489. D: 489. II. A1: 489; WES.

Munzinger, Werner, 1864, *Ostafrikanische Studien*, Schaffhausen, F. Hurter.

Kurtatchi (ca. 1930) I. A: 60. B: 291. C1 and C2: 85. C3: 45, 109. C4: 105. C5: 60-61, 85, 88. D: 440, 453, 454. II. A1: 23, 51, 59. A2: 114. A3: 260. A4: 269-70. B: 75. C: 77, 78. D: 60, 64.

Blackwood, Beatrice, 1935, *Both sides of Buka Passage: an ethnographic study of social, sexual, and economic questions in the north-western Solomon Islands*, Oxford, Clarendon Press.

Kutchin (ca. 1932) I. A: 113. B: 113, 116. C1 and C2: 141. C3: 151. C4: 144. C5: 113, 116. D: 110, 113. II. A1: 143, 148. A2: 144. A3: 109, 110. A4: 141, 150-51. B: 142. D: 116.

Osgood, Cornelius, 1936, "Contributions to the ethnography of the Kutchin," *Yale University Publications in Anthropology 14.*

Lakalai (ca. 1964) I. A: (a) 494. B: (a) 486, 494. C1 and C2: (a) 492. C3: (a) 492, 493. C4: (a) 486. C5: (a) 487, 488. D: (a)491. II. A1: (a)488, 493. A2: (b)451. A3: (a)495; (b)443. A4: (b)451. B: (a)485. C: (a)478, 484, 487. D: (a)486, 488.

(a) Chowning, Ann, 1965-66, "Lakalai kinship," *Anthropological Forum 1:* 476-501.

(b) Valentine, Charles A., 1963, "Men of anger and men of shame: Lakalai ethnopsychology and its implications for sociopsychological theory," *Ethnology 2:* 441-77.

Lake Shore Tonga (2d quarter, 20th C.) I. A: 55, 105, 106, 141. B: 141. C1 and C2: 85, 92. C3: 55, 151. C5: 50, 83, 87. D: 105. II. A1: 123. A2: 123. A3: 170, 216. B: 128, 139, 182.

Van Velsen, J., 1964, *The politics of kinship*, Manchester, published on behalf of the Rhodes-Livingstone Institute by Manchester University Press.

Lele (2d quarter, 20th C.) I. A: (a)96, 196. B: (a)119, 124; (b)3. C1 and C2: (a)34, 36, 59, 119. C3: (a)152, 176. C4: (a)20. C5: (a)114, 115. D: (a)30, 52, 122. II. A1: (a)118, 122, 128, 136ff. A2: (a)76, 98, 121-23. A3: (a)197. A4: (a)34, 207. B: (a)35, 114. C: (a)199, 202. D: (a)124.

(a) Douglas, Mary, 1963, *The Lele of the Kasai*, London, published for the International African Institute by Oxford University Press.

(b) Tew, Mary, 1951, "A form of polyandry among the Lele of the Kasai," *Africa 21:* 1-12.

Lesu (2d quarter, 20th C.) I. A: 252, 253, 257. B: 29, 53. C1 and C2: 145, 146. C3: 32, 262. C4: 53, 255. C5: 91. D: 157-58, 167. II. A1: 226, 228. A2: 144, 228, 244, 245. A3: 58, 297. A4: 143. B: 50-51. C: 40-41, 52. D: 53.

Powdermaker, Hortense, 1933, *Life in Lesu: the study of a Melanesian society in New Ireland*, New York, Norton.

Lobi (1st quarter, 20th C.) I. A: 281, 282, 283. B: 252, 342. C1 and C2: 264, 268, 279. C3: 281. C4: 281. C5: 249, 251. D: 283. II. A1: 251, 261, 280, 285. A2: 286, 377-78. A3: 462, plate 29. A4: 284-85. B: 262. C: 259-60.

Labouret, Henri, 1931, "Les tribus du rameau lobi," *Paris, Université, Institut d'Ethnologie, Travaux et Mémoires 15.*

Locono (15th C.) I. C2: (a)531. C5: (a)532. II. A1: (a)531; WES. A3: (a)529, 534. B: (b) 284, 289.

(a) Rouse, Irving, 1948, "The Arawak," *U.S. BAE, Bulletin 143, vol. 4:* 507-46 (secondary source).

(b) Taylor, Douglas Macrae, 1957, "Marriage, affinity, and descent in two Arawakan tribes: a sociolinguistic note," *IJAL 23:* 284-90.

Longudu (2d quarter, 20th C.) I. A: 347. C1: 349. C2: 347, 348. C3: 341. C4: 335. C5: 341. II. A1: 337. B: 340, 341.

Meek, Charles K., 1931, "The Longuda," in his *Tribal Studies in Northern Nigeria, vol. 2,* London, Kegan Paul, Trench, Trübner: 331-68.

Luguru (2d quarter, 20th C.) I. A: (a) 1316,.1317; (d)60.
B: (a)1316. C1: (b)259. C2: (b)259-60; (c)71. C3: (a)1319;
(c)77. C5: (a)1315. D: (c)57-58, 61. II. A1: (a)1326;
(b)246; (c)57. A2: (a)1320. A3: (c)53. A4: (b)262. B:
(a)1316. C: (a)1321, 1326. D: (a)1316.

(a) Christensen, James B., 1963, "Utani: joking, sexual
license and social obligations among the Luguru, *AA*
65: 1314-27.

(b) Scheerder and Tastevin, Les R.R.P.P., 1950, "Les
Wa lu guru (Tanganyika)," *Anthropos 45:* 241-86.

(c) Young, Roland, and Henry Fosbrooke, 1960, *Smoke
in the hills,* Evanston, Northwestern University Press.

(d) Wallis, P., 1934, "Waluguru sibs," *Primitive Man 7:*
58-63.

Majuro (early 20th C.) I. A: 195, 198. B: 134, 190. C1 and
C2: 214. C3: 115. C5: 194, 197. D: 115. II. A1: 76-77.
A2: 215, 222. A3: 156, 169. A4: 113. B: 204. C: 178,
179, 196, 214. D: 195, 199.

Spoehr, Alexander, 1949, "Majuro: a village in the Mar-
shall Islands," *Fieldiana: Anthropology 39.*

Mesakin (1st quarter, 20th C.) I. A: (a)291; (b)384. C1 and
C2: (a)286. C3: (a)29. C4: (a)308; (b)385. C5: (a)273. D:
(a)293. II. A1: (a)285, 315; (b)388; WES. A2: (a)289; (b)
385. A3: (a)308. A4: (a)272, 284; (b)368, 386. B: (a)282;
(b)383. C: (a)282, 285.

(a) Nadel, Siegfried F., 1947, *The Nuba,* London, Oxford University Press.

(b) Seligman, Charles G., and Brenda Z. Seligman,
1932, *Pagan tribes of the Nilotic Sudan,* London,
George Routledge and Sons.

Minangkabau (late 19th C.—early 20th C.) I. A: (b)10;
(c)111. B: (a)49; (b)101. C1 and C2: (a)46; (b)65. C3:
(c)112. C4: (a)36; (c)110. C5: (c)110, 117. D: (b)56;

(c)106. II. A1: (a)44. A2: (a)36. A3: (c)119. A4: (a)43. B: (b)11. C: (c)110, 113. D: (c)113.

(a) Loeb, Edwin M., 1934, "Patrilineal and matrilineal organization in Sumatra: Part 2. The Minangkabau," *AA, n.s. 36:* 26-56.

(b) Loeb, Edwin M., 1935, "Sumatra: its history and people," *Wiener Beiträge zur Kulturgeschichte und Linguistik 3:* 1-303.

(c) Josselin de Jong, Patrick E. de, 1952, *Minangkabau and Negri Sembilan: socio-political structure in Indonesia,* Leiden, Eduard Ijdo (secondary source).

Mnong Gar (ca. 1949) I. A: (a)30, 31. B: (a)314. C1 and C2: (a)189, 196-97. C4: (a)99, 314. C5: (a)30, 196. D: (a)30. II. A1: (a)227; (b)21. A2: (a)136-37. A3: (a)29, 34. A4: (a)172, 433. B: (a)381, 460. C: (a)99, 100. D: (a)99.

(a) Condominas, Georges, 1957, *Nous avons mangé la forêt,* Paris, Mercure de France.

(b) Condominas, Georges, 1960, "The Mnong Gar of Central Vietnam," *Viking Fund Publications in Anthropology 29:* 15-23.

Mota (late 19th C.—early 20th C.) I. A: (b)41, 44. B: (a)43; (b) 40-41. C1 and C2: (a)240. C3: (a)244. C4: (a)243; (b)44. C5: (a)231. D: (a)110; (b)58. II. A1: (a)40, 236, 245-46. A2: (a)243. A3: (b)72, 135, 139. B: (a)29; (b)48, 50. C: (a)43; (b)50. D: (b)36.

(a) Rivers, William H. R., 1914, *The history of Melanesian society, vol. 1,* Cambridge, University Press.

(b) Codrington, R. H., 1891, *The Melanesians: studies in their anthropology and folklore,* Oxford, Clarendon Press.

Nambicuara (2d quarter, 20th C.) I. A: (a)99; (c)44. B: (b)173, 180; (c)45-46. C1 and C2: (b)104. [C4: (d)111.] C5: (a)99. D: (a)99. II. A1: (a)96; (c)44; WES. [A2:

(d)111.]   A3:   (b)172, 175.   [A4:   (d)63.]   B: (a)99. C:
(b)178. D: (b)172.

(a) Oberg, Kalervo, 1953, "Indian tribes of northern
Mato Grosso, Brazil," *Smithsonian Institution, Institute
of Social Anthropology, Publication 15.*

(b) Lévi-Strauss, Claude, 1968, "The social use of kinship terms among Brazilian Indians," in Paul Bohannan
and John Middleton, eds., *Marriage, Family, and Residence*, Garden City, Natural History Press: 169-84.

(c) Roquette-Pinto, E., 1938, "Rondonia," *Biblioteca
Pedagogica Brasileira, ser. 5: Brasiliana 39* (HRAF
1959).

[(d) Lévi-Strauss, Claude, 1948, "La vie familiale et
sociale des Indiens Nambikwara," *Journal, Société des
Americanistes 37:* 1-131. (These codings were done too
late to use for, tests of association. Their inclusion
would not alter the results significantly.)]

Nauru (2d quarter, 20th C.) I. A: 383. B: 381. C1 and C2:
389. C3: 390. C4: 380. C5: 376. D: 20-23. II. A1: 383,
390. A2: 380, 390. A3: 377, 385. B: 382. D: 380.

Wedgwood, Camilla H., 1936, "Report on anthropological research work in Nauru Island, Central Pacific,"
Oceania 6: 359-91; *7:* 1-33.

Nayar (ca. 1949) I. A: 345, 355. B: 352, 363, 368. C1 and
C2: 328. C3: 346, 359, 360, 368. C4: 340, 362. C5: 350,
364. D: 335, 341. II. A1: 358, 367, 369, 370. A2: 329,
362. A3: 355. A4: 330, 331, 356. B: 352, 368. C: 352,
368. D: 351, 368.

Gough, Kathleen, 1961, "Nayar: Central Kerala," in
David M. Schneider and Kathleen Gough, eds., *Matrilineal Kinship*, Berkeley, University of California Press:
298-384.

Ndembu (ca. 1954) I. A: (a)78, 123, 244, 248-49. B:
(a)248-49; (b)210, 249, 257. C1 and C2: (a)265; (b)262,

263. C3: (a)51, 52, 62, 123. C4: (a)120. C5: (a)189, 237, 241-42. D: (a)23. II. A1: (a)281; (b)267. A2: (b)149. A3: (a)293; (c)159. A4: (b)248; (c)78, 154. B: (a)243. C: (a)86, 248, 252. D: (a)235, 240.

(a) Turner, Victor, 1957, *Schism and continuity in an African society*, Manchester, published on behalf of the Rhodes-Livingstone Institute by Manchester University Press.

(b) Turner, Victor, 1967, *The forest of symbols*, Ithaca, Cornell University Press.

(c) Turner, Victor, 1968, *The drums of affliction*, Oxford, Clarendon Press.

Palau (early 19th C.) I. A: (a)24, 26, 62. B: (a)139, 179, 181, 215. C1 and C2: (a) 132, 133. C3: (a)142. C4: (a)179, 182. C5: (a)26, 27, 33. D: (a)63. II. A1: (a)141, 145. A2: (a)142. A3: (a)181, 182; (b)40, 53. B: (a)28. C: (a)23, 28. D: (a)123.

(a) Barnett, Homer G., 1949, *Palauan society*, Eugene, University of Oregon Publications.

(b) Force, Roland W., 1960, "Leadership and culture change in Palau," *Fieldiana: Anthropology 50.*

Pawnee (late 19th C.) I. A: (a)27, 28. B: (a)25, 35. C1: (a)17. C2: (c)276, 279. C4: (a)25, 43. C5: (a)17, 24, 25. D: (a)37, 45. II. A1: (a)16, 17, 25, 34. A2: (a)43; (b)109. A3: (a)45, 96, 99, 379. A4: (b)80, 95-96. B: (a)24, 25. D: (a)18, 35.

(a) Weltfish, Gene, 1965, *The lost universe*, New York, Basic Books.

(b) Grinnell, George B., 1891, "Marriage among the Pawnees," *AA 4:* 275-81.

(c) Dorsey, George A., and James R. Murie, 1940, "Notes on Skidi Pawnee society," *Chicago, Field Museum of Natural History, Anthropology Series 27, no. 2:* 65-119.

Plateau Tonga (ca. 1950) I. A: 48, 100, 105, 140. B: 58, 141, 145, 251. C1: 337. C2: 102, 330. C3: 182, 183. C4: 142, 145, 251. C5: 224. D: 109, 113, 116. II. A1: 120, 123. A2: 164, 165-66. A3: 104. A4: 139. B: 326. C: 321. D: 58, 251.

Colson, Elizabeth, 1958, *Marriage and the family among the Plateau Tonga of northern Rhodesia*, Manchester, published on behalf of the Institute for Social Research, University of Zambia, by Manchester University Press.

Ponape (before 1912) I. A: (a)135, 148. B: (a)134, 135, 195. C1 and C2: (a)121, 122. C3: (a)123. C5: (a)123, 134. D: (a)142-43, 148. II. A1: (a)124. A2: (a)123, 124, 194. A3: (a)178. B: (a)122, 176. C: (a)114, 122; (b)213. D: (a)133, 134.

(a) Fischer, John L., with the assistance of Ann M. Fischer, 1957, *The Eastern Carolines*, New Haven, HRAF Press.

(b) Garvin, Paul L., and Saul H. Riesenberg, 1952, "Respect behavior on Ponape: an ethnolinguistic study," *AA 54:* 201-20.

Rhade (ca. 1950) I. A: 29, 46. C1 and C2: 26, 27. C4: 29. C5: 30, 31. D: 28, 46, 80, 92. II. A1: 28. A2: 28. A3: 29, 46, 81. B: 24. D: 30.

Donoghue, John D., Daniel D. Whitney, and Iwao Ishino, 1962, *People in the middle: the Rhade of South Viet Nam*, East Lansing, Michigan State University (mimeographed).

Rossel Island (ca. 1920) I. A: 95-96, 100. C1: 93, 94. C2: 87, 93-97. C3: 94, 100. C4: 100. C5: 93, 184. D: 69. II. A1: 97; WES. A2: 98. A3: 179ff. A4: 101. B: 43, 44. C: 128, 132. D: 55.

Armstrong, W. E., 1928, *Rossel Island*, Cambridge, at the University Press.

Santa Cruz (2d quarter, 20th C.) coded by ethnographer, William Davenport.

Saramacca (ca. 1929) I. A: (a)140; (b)120. B: (a)155, 191. C1 and C2: (b)122. C3: (a)130. C4: (a)155. C5: (a)128, 129, 135, 140. D: (b) 132. II. A1: (a)131, 159. A2: (a)74; (b)121, 124. A3: (a)82, 159, 163-65, 192. A4: (a)154, 319; (b)130. B: (c)718. C: (c)718. D: (a)143, 208.

> (a) Herskovits, Melville J., and Frances S. Herskovits, 1934, *Rebel destiny: among the Bush Negroes of Dutch Guiana*, New York, McGraw-Hill.
>
> (b) Kahn, Morton C., 1931, *Djuka: the Bush Negroes of Dutch Guiana*, New York, Viking Press.
>
> (c) Herskovits, Melville J., 1930, "The social organization of the Bush-Negroes of Suriname," *International Congress of Americanists, Proceedings, 23:* 713-27.

Sherbro (2d quarter, 20th C.) I. A: (a)3. B: (a)14. C1 and C2: (a)3. C5: (a)3. II. A1: (a)4. A2: (b)83. A3: (a)4, 6. B: (a)3. C: (a)3.

> (a) McCulloch, Merran, 1950, *Peoples of Sierra Leone Protectorate*, London, International African Institute.
>
> (b) Hall, Henry U., 1938, *The Sherbro of Sierra Leone*, Philadelphia, University Press, University of Pennsylvania.

Siriono (ca. 1941) I. A: 49, 50. B: 49, 57, 59. C1 and C2: 82. C3: 50, 61. C4: 50, 60. C5: 49. D: 59, 62. II. A1: 168, 215. A2: 60-62. A4: 170-71. B: 168, 214. C: 54, 64. D: 56, 57.

> Holmberg, Allan R., 1950, "Nomads of the long bow: the Siriono of eastern Bolivia," *Smithsonian Institution, Institute of Social Anthropology, Publication 10.*

Siuai (ca. 1938) I. A: 167, 168, 228, 259. B: 156, 157, 235, 261. C1: 154. C2: 155, 156, 161, 162, 285, 287. C3: 240. C4: 197, 223. C5: 195, 199, 257, 284. D: 205, 216.

II. A1: 223. A2: 142, 442. A3: 159, 238-39, 458. A4:
201, 204. B: 153. C: 248, 255, 442-43. D: 207, 235.

Oliver, Douglas, 1955, *A Solomon Island society*, Cambridge, Harvard University Press.

Suku (ca. 1958) I. A: (a)102. C1 and C2: (a)197; (b)474.
C3: (a)102. C5: (a)97, 103, 104. D: (a)101; (b)454. II. A1:
(a)90, 105. A3: (b)460-61, 471. B: (a)100. C: (b)452.

(a) Kopytoff, Igor, 1965, "The Suku of southwestern
Congo," in James L. Gibbs, ed., *Peoples of Africa*, New
York, Holt, Rinehart and Winston: 441-77.

(b) Kopytoff, Igor, 1964, "Family and lineage among
the Suku of the Congo," in Robert F. Gray and Philip
H. Gulliver, eds., *The Family Estate in Africa*, Boston,
Boston University Press: 83-116.

Talamanca (late 19th C.—early 20th C.) I. A: (a)34. B:
(a)34. C1 and C2: (a)34. C4: (b)496. C5: (a)29. D: (a)40.
II. A1: (a)29. A2: (b)496. A3: (b)507-10. A4: (a)27. B:
(a)35. C: (a)35; (b)496, 497. D: (a)28.

(a) Stone, Doris Z., 1962, "The Talamancan tribes of
Costa Rica," *Harvard University, Peabody Museum of
Archaeology and Ethnology, Papers 43, no. 2.*

(b) Gabb, William M., 1876, "On the Indian tribes and
languages of Costa Rica," *American Philosophical Society, Proceedings 14:* 483-602.

Tanaina (ca. 1931) I. A: (a)137-38; (b)709. B: (a)137. C1
and C2: (a)164-65. C3: (a)141. C5: (a)143; (b)710. D:
(a)137, 138; (b)709, 710. II. A1: (a)165. A2: (a)165. A3:
(a)138. A4: (a)160, 162, 174; (b)713. B: (a)164.

(a) Osgood, Cornelius, 1937, "The ethnography of the
Tanaina," *Yale University Publications in Anthropology
16.*

(b) Osgood, Cornelius, 1933, "Tanaina culture," *AA, n.s.
35:* 695-717.

Timbira (ca. 1936) I. A: 125. B: 113, 125, 157. C1 and
C2: 124. C3: 124. C4: 113. C5: 124, 125, 165. D: 59, 70,
75, 113, 157. II. A1: 120. A2: 104, 107, 119, 128. A3:
84, 92, 97, 120. A4: 121. B: 124. C: 122, 124. D: 53,
125, 131.

Nimuendajú, Curt, 1946, "The Eastern Timbira," *California, University, Publications in American Archaeology and Ethnology 41.*

Tiwi (ca. 1929) I. A: (a)45, 53. B: (a)45, 53. C1: (c)460.
C2: (a)20. C3: no divorce mentioned. C4: (a)53; (b)252.
C5: (a)45. D: (a)33, 36. II. A1: (b)244. A2: (b)246. B:
(c)454-55. D: (a)53.

(a) Hart, Charles William Merton, and Arnold R. Pilling,
1960, *The Tiwi of North Australia*, New York, Holt.

(b) Hart, Charles William Merton, 1954, "The sons of
Turimpi," *AA 56:* 242-61.

(c) Goodale, Jane C., 1962, "Marriage contracts among
the Tiwi," *Ethnology 1:* 452-66.

Tlingit (ca. 1880) I. A: (d)1. B: (b)424; (d)1; (e)27. C1
and C2: (a)153-54; (b)152. C4: (c)148, 149. C5: (a)10. D:
(c)145, 149. II. A1: (a)154; (c)148. A2: (a)155; (c)148.
A3: (a)164-68. A4: (a)153. B: (e)64, 65. C: (c)146. D:
(d)1, 2; (e)33, 36.

(a) Krause, Aurel, 1956, *The Tlingit Indians: results of
a trip to the Northwest Coast of America and the Bering Straits*, Seattle, University of Washington Press for
the American Ethnological Society.

(b) Swanton, John R., 1908, "Social condition, beliefs,
and linguistic relationship of the Tlingit Indians," *U.S.
BAE, Annual Report 26:* 391-486.

(c) Oberg, Kalervo, 1934, "Crime and punishment in
Tlingit society," *AA, n.s. 36:* 145-55.

(d) Soboieff, Walter, n.d., *Tlingit culture* (mimeographed).

(e) Durlach, Theresa Mayer, 1928, "The relationship systems of the Tlingit, Haida, and Tsimshian," *American Ethnological Society, Publication 11.*

Trobriand Islands (1st quarter, 20th C.) I. A: (a)18, 129; (b)25; (e)35. B: (a)18, 521; (c)61, 75, 180; (e)35. C1 and C2: (a)93. C3: (a)98, 120. C4: (a)107, 119-20, 142-43. C5: (a)18, 129. D: (a)25, 129. II. A1: (a)130, 137, 138. A2: (a)115, 119-20. A3: (a)34, 36, 179. A4: (a)169. B: (a)95, 101. C: (a)62, 87, 528, 531-32, 566; (d)90. D: (c)71.

(a) Malinowski, Bronislaw, 1929, *The sexual life of savages in Northwest Melanesia*, 2 vols., New York, Horace Liveright.

(b) Malinowski, Bronislaw, 1953, *Sex and repression in savage society*, London, Routledge and Kegan Paul (originally published in 1927).

(c) Malinowski, Bronislaw, 1922, *Argonauts of the Western Pacific*, London, George Routledge and Sons.

(d) Fortune, Reo, 1932, *Sorcerers of Dobu*, London, Routledge.

(e) Malinowski, Bronislaw, 1926, *Crime and custom in savage society*, London and New York, Kegan Paul, Trench, Trübner; Harcourt, Brace.

Truk (before 1902) I. A: (b)469-70. B: (a)113; (b)469-70. C1 and C2: (a)121. C3: (b)469-70. C4: (b)471, 473. C5: (a)31-33. D: (a)31-34; (b)471. II. A1: (a)122-23. A2: (a)122; (c)532. A3: (b)471. A4: (c)531, 538. B: (a)121. C: (a)117, 120. D: (a)113, 117.

(a) Goodenough, Ward H., 1951, "Property, kin, and community on Truk," *Yale University Publications in Anthropology 46.*

(b) Swartz, Marc J., 1958, "Sexuality and aggression on Romonum, Truk," *AA 60:* 467-86.

(c) Fischer, Ann, 1963, "Reproduction on Truk," *Ethnology 2:* 526-40.

Tsimshian (early 20th C.) I. A: (a)268; (b)22. C1 and C2: (a)233; (b)24. C3: (b)24. C5: (a)324, 325. D: (a)275, 276; (b)14, 15, 17, 23. II. A1: (a)234, 235. A3: (a)203, 262; (b)16, 28. A4: (b)40, 122. B: (a)230, 231. D: (a)326, 327.

(a) Garfield, Viola, 1939, "Tsimshian clan and society," *University of Washington Publications in Anthropology 7, no. 3:* 169-339.

(b) Garfield, Viola, et al., 1951, "The Tsimshian: their arts and music," *American Ethnological Society, Publication 18.*

Tuareg (Ahaggar) (2d quarter, 20th C.) I. A: (a)475. B: (a)448, 475. C1 and C2: (a)460. C3: (a)142-43; (b)586. C4: (b)154. C5: (a)400, 468. D: (a)136, 210. II. A1: WES. A2: (b)154. A3: no mention of any positions. A4: (a)126, 204; (b)144. B: (a)458. C: (a)464. D: no mention of any avoidance.

(a) Nicolaisen, Johannes, 1963, "Ecology and culture of the Pastoral Tuareg," *Copenhagen, Nationalmuseets Skrifter, Etnografisk Raekke 9.*

(b) Lhote, Henri, 1944, *Les Touaregs du Hoggar*, Paris, Payot.

Vedda ("*Wild*") (early 20th C.) I. A: 88, 89. B: 88. C1 and C2: 95, 97-98. C3: 100. C5: 67. D: 112, 118. II. A1: 87. A2: 87. A3: 249, no mention of any. A4: 94. B: 64, 97. C: 65, 75. D: 68-69.

Seligmann, Charles G., and Brenda Z. Seligmann, 1911, *The Veddas*, Cambridge, University Press.

Yao (ca. 1949) I. A: (a)316-17, 325, 331; (b)144. B: (a)329. C1 and C2: (a)325. C3: (a)326, 328, 330. C4: (a)151. C5: (a)316-17, 320. D: (a)62-63. II. A1: (a)341. A2: (a)326. A3: (b)161. A4: (c)288. B: (b)197. C: (b)146. D: (a)328, 330.

(a) Mitchell, James Clyde, 1959, "The Yao of southern

Nyasaland," in Elizabeth Colson and Max Gluckman, eds., *Seven Tribes of British Central Africa* (corrected reprint), Manchester, published on behalf of the Rhodes-Livingstone Institute by Manchester University Press: 292-353.

(b) Mitchell, James Clyde, 1956, *The Yao village: a study in the social structure of a Nyasaland tribe*, Manchester, published on behalf of the Rhodes-Livingstone Institute by Manchester University Press.

(c) Stannus, Hugh S., 1922, "The Wayao of Nyasaland," *Harvard African Studies 3:* 229-372.

Yavapai (Keweyipaya) (early 20th C.) I. A: 197. B: 195, 197. C1 and C2: 195-96. C3: 190. C4: 197. C5: 198. II. A1: 196. A2: 197. A3: 197, 204, 236, 238. A4: 192, 215. B: 195. C: 190, 195. D: 195.

Gifford, Edward W., 1932, "The Southeastern Yavapai," *California, University, Publications in American Archaeology and Ethnology 29, no. 3.*

Appendix C: Code Book

Variables

1. World Area
   1—Africa (plus Guanche of Tenerife)
   2—Asia (including Belu and Minangkabau)
   3—Oceania
   4—South America
   5—North America

2. Sex of Major Researcher
   1—male
   2—female

3. Quantity of Data
   1—poorly reported (under 100 pages)
   2—adequately reported (100-250 pages)
   3—well reported (over 250 pages, or shorter but with detailed reports on kinship and family life)

4. Domestic Authority Pattern
   1—strong husband dominance
   2—lesser husband dominance
   3—neither dominant
   4—lesser brother dominance
   5—strong brother dominance

5. Wife Defers to Husband
   1—absent
   2—present

6. Sister Defers to Brother
   1—absent
   2—present

7. Husband Defers to Wife's Brother or Mother's Brother
   1—absent
   2—present

8. Brother Defers to Sister's Husband
   1—absent
   2—present

9. Bride Capture
   1—absent
   2—present

10. Bridewealth
    1—absent
    2—present: substantial
    3—present: token

11. Bride Service
    1—absent
    2—present: substantial
    3—present: token

12. Woman Exchange
    1—absent
    2—present

13. Divorce
    1—absent
    2—present: wife leaves
    3—present: husband leaves
    4—present: other pattern

14. Marriage Disruption by Wife's Brother or Mother's Brother
    1—absent
    2—present

15. Marriage Disruption by Outsiders in Another Form
    1—absent
    2—present

16. Aggression of Husband Against Wife Tolerated
    1—absent
    2—present

17. Aggression of Brother Against Sister Tolerated
    1—absent
    2—present

18. Control Over Children by Men
    1—absent: mother has control
    2—present: father has control
    3—present: mother's brother has control
    4—present: control shared by father and mother's
    brother

19. Control Over Domestic Group Property
    1—absent: no property common to the domestic group
    2—present: husband control
    3—present: husband and wife share control
    4—present: wife control
    5—present: brother and sister share control
    6—present: brother control
    7—present: husband and brother share control

20. Polygyny
    1—absent
    2—present: limited
    3—present: general

21. Sororal Polygyny Discussed in Report
    1—absent
    2—present: no preference for or against sororal polyg-
    yny
    3—present: preference for sororal polygyny
    4—present: preference against sororal polygyny

22. Co-Wife Jealousy
    1—absent
    2—present

23. Polyandry Allowed
    1—absent
    2—present

24. Adultery Allowed for Husband
    1—absent
    2—present

25. Adultery Allowed for Wife
    1—absent
    2—present

26. Wife Is Punished for Adultery
    1—absent
    2—present: by husband or his kin group
    3—present: by brother or her kin group
    4—present: by other means

27. Husband Can Dispose of Wife's Sexuality without Her Consent
    1—absent
    2—present

28. Women Hold Ascribed Positions Exclusive to Women
    1—absent
    2—present

29. Women Hold Achieved Positions Exclusive to Women
    1—absent
    2—present

30. Women Hold Ascribed Positions Also Held by Men
    1—absent
    2—present

31. Women Hold Achieved Positions Also Held by Men
    1—absent
    2—present

32. Groups of Women Perform Publicly
    1—absent
    2—present

33. Menstrual Restrictions
    1—absent
    2—present: menstrual seclusion
    3—present: taboo on food preparation
    4—present: other restrictions
    5—present: only restriction is on sexual intercourse

34. Menstrual Restrictions Are Said to Protect Women
    1—absent
    2—present

35. Menstrual Restrictions Are Said to Protect People and/ or Objects against the Menstruant
    1—absent
    2—present

36. Menstrual Blood Endangers Ritual Objects and/or Spiritual Power
    1—absent
    2—present

37. Menstrual Blood Endangers the Food Supply
    1—absent
    2—present

38. Menstrual Blood Harms Men Who Come into Contact with It
    1—absent
    2—present

39. Preferential Marriage (Male Ego)
    1—absent: no single-category preference as codeable here
    2—present: patrilateral parallel cousin
    3—present: matrilateral cross-cousin
    4—present: patrilateral cross-cousin
    5—present: female linked to Ego through his mother
    6—present: female linked to Ego through his father
           (there were no such cases reported)

40. Direction of the Incest Taboo
    1—absent: no such cases recorded
    2—present: sibling incest worse than father-daughter
    3—present: sibling incest equal to father-daughter
    4—present: sibling incest milder than father-daughter

41. Severity of Sibling Incest Sanctions
    1—absent
    2—sibling incest permitted under certain conditions
    3—sibling incest bad, but no immediate sanctions
    4—sibling incest bad, mildly punished

5—sibling incest bad, severely punished

42. Nonextension of Sibling Incest Taboos to Classificatory Siblings
    1—absent: sibling incest taboos broadly extended
    2—present: marriage prohibited, but sexual relations allowed
    3—present: marriage allowed

43. Brother-Sister Avoidance
    1—absent
    2—present: total
    3—present: partial

44. Father-Daughter Avoidance
    1—absent
    2—present: total
    3—present: partial

45. Intensity of Agriculture
    1—absent
    2—present: casual
    3—present: shifting
    4—present: horticulture
    5—present: intensive

46. Intensity of Animal Use
    1—absent: no domesticated animals
    2—present: domesticated animals, nonherding economy
    3—present: herding or intensive animal harvesting

47. Intensive Trade
    1—absent
    2—present

48. Craft Specialization
    1—absent
    2—present: minimal
    3—present: intensive

49. Social Stratification Scale
    1—absent
    2—present: low
    3—present: medium
    4—present: high

50. Political Integration Scale
    1—absent: political integration minimal
    2—present: low
    3—present: medium
    4—present: high

51. Spatial Mobility
    1—absent
    2—present: low
    3—present: medium
    4—present: high

52. Wife-Centered Residence of Domestic Group
    1—absent: husband-centered or other-centered
    2—present: uxorilocal
    3—present: matrilocal
    4—present: avunculocal, with preference for matri-
      lateral cross-cousin marriage

53. Husband-Centered Residence of Domestic Group
    1—absent: wife-centered or other-centered
    2—present: virilocal
    3—present: patrilocal
    4—present: avunculocal, without preference for matri-
      lateral cross-cousin marriage

54. Other Residential Type
    1—absent: husband-centered or wife-centered
    2—present: neolocal or ambilocal
    3—present: duolocal

55. Quality of Data
    1—low reliability: under one year, no native language
    2—medium reliability: under one year with native lan-
      guage, or one year or longer without native lan-
      guage
    3—high reliability: one year or longer with native lan-
      guage

Appendix D: Code Sheet

Codes for Societies

1. Ambo	24. Kurtatchi	45. Plateau Tonga
2. Ashanti	25. Kutchin	46. Ponape
3. Aua	26. Lakalai	47. Rhade
4. Belu	27. Lake Shore	48. Rossel Island
5. Bemba	Tonga	49. Santa Cruz
6. Bororo	28. Lele	50. Saramacca
7. Callinago	29. Lesu	51. Sherbro
8. Cochiti	30. Lobi	52. Siriono
9. Coniagui	31. Luguru	53. Siuai
10. Creek	32. Locono	54. Suku
11. Crow	33. Longudu	55. Talamanca
12. Darfur	34. Majuro	56. Tanaina
13. Delaware	35. Mesakin	57. Timbira
14. Dieri	36. Minangkabau	58. Tiwi
15. Garo	37. Mnong Gar	59. Tlingit
16. Goajiro	38. Mota	60. Trobriand
17. Guanche	39. Nambicuara	Islands
18. Gure	40. Nauru	61. Truk
19. Hopi	41. Nayar	62. Tsimshian
20. Iroquois	42. Ndembu	63. Tuareg
21. Kaska	43. Palau	64. Vedda
22. Khasi	44. Pawnee	65. Yavapai
23. Kunama		66. Yao

Note: Each number in the first column on the code sheet refers to a society. Numbers at the head of subsequent columns refer to variables, beginning with Variable 4, Domestic Authority Pattern, in the Code Book, Appendix C. The number 9 means *no information*.

	4	5	6	7	8	9	10	11	12	13	14	15	16	17	18	19	20	21	22	23	24	25	26	27	28
1.	2	1	9	9	9	2	3	9	9	2	1	1	2	9	2	2	3	4	1	1	2	1	2	1	9
2.	4	2	2	9	9	1	3	1	1	2	2	1	9	9	3	7	3	3	1	1	2	1	9	9	2
3.	5	9	9	9	9	1	1	1	3	9	1	9	9	3	6	3	2	1	9	9	9	9	9	9	9
4.	3	1	9	9	1	1	3	3	1	3	9	2	1	9	3	4	2	9	2	1	1	1	1	1	9
5.	2	2	1	1	1	1	3	2	1	3	1	9	2	1	4	2	2	3	2	1	2	1	2	1	9
6.	4	2	2	9	9	9	9	9	9	3	9	9	9	9	9	3	2	3	9	1	9	9	9	9	9
7.	1	2	9	1	1	1	1	1	1	3	1	2	2	9	2	9	2	3	2	1	9	1	3	9	9
8.	3	1	9	9	9	1	1	1	1	3	1	1	1	9	2	3	1	1	1	1	1	1	1	1	2
9.	2	2	2	9	9	1	1	3	1	2	9	9	2	9	2	2	3	9	9	1	2	1	2	9	2
10.	4	2	2	9	9	1	3	1	1	3	2	9	2	2	3	4	2	3	1	1	1	2	9	1	1
11.	2	2	1	1	1	1	2	1	1	2	1	2	2	1	2	2	3	3	2	1	2	2	2	2	9
12.	1	2	2	9	9	1	2	1	2	3	9	9	2	9	2	3	2	9	2	1	2	2	2	9	2
13.	3	9	9	9	9	1	3	1	1	3	9	9	9	9	3	3	2	9	2	1	2	1	2	9	2
14.	1	1	9	1	1	2	1	1	2	2	9	9	2	9	2	9	2	3	2	1	2	2	1	2	1
15.	4	2	2	1	1	1	1	1	1	3	2	9	2	2	3	4	2	4	2	1	1	1	3	1	1
16.	2	2	1	9	9	1	2	1	1	2	2	2	1	1	3	3	2	9	2	1	9	1	3	9	1
17.	2	9	9	9	9	1	1	1	1	2	1	1	9	9	2	9	1	1	1	1	9	1	9	2	9
18.	4	9	9	9	9	1	1	1	9	2	2	9	9	9	3	9	2	9	9	1	2	2	9	9	9
19.	3	1	1	1	1	1	1	1	1	3	1	1	1	1	4	4	1	1	1	1	2	2	1	1	2
20.	3	2	1	9	9	1	1	1	3	1	2	1	9	1	3	1	1	1	1	1	1	1	1	1	2
21.	2	2	1	1	1	1	1	2	1	3	9	9	2	9	2	3	2	3	2	2	1	1	2	2	1
22.	4	2	9	9	9	1	1	1	3	2	1	2	9	3	5	2	4	1	1	2	1	2	1	2	2
23.	2	9	9	9	9	1	3	1	1	2	1	1	2	1	2	2	9	9	1	9	9	9	9	9	9
24.	4	1	1	9	9	1	3	1	1	4	1	1	2	9	3	3	3	2	2	9	1	1	3	9	9
25.	3	1	1	1	1	1	1	1	1	2	1	9	2	1	1	3	2	2	1	2	9	9	2	9	1
26.	2	9	1	1	1	1	2	1	2	2	1	9	9	1	2	2	2	2	2	1	2	2	9	9	1
27.	2	2	9	9	9	1	2	1	1	3	2	2	9	9	4	2	2	9	9	1	2	1	2	1	1
28.	2	2	1	9	9	2	2	1	2	2	2	2	2	1	2	3	3	4	2	2	1	1	2	2	9
29.	3	1	1	9	9	1	3	1	1	3	1	1	2	1	2	3	2	9	9	2	2	2	1	1	9
30.	2	2	9	2	1	1	3	2	9	2	1	2	2	9	2	2	3	2	1	1	2	1	2	9	1
31.	4	9	9	1	1	1	2	1	1	3	2	1	9	9	3	3	2	4	9	1	1	9	9	9	9
32.	9	9	9	9	9	9	2	2	9	9	9	9	9	9	2	9	2	3	9	1	9	9	9	9	9
33.	9	9	9	9	9	2	2	2	1	2	9	9	2	9	3	9	3	9	9	9	9	9	9	9	9
34.	3	1	1	1	1	1	1	1	4	9	9	9	9	2	3	2	9	9	1	2	2	1	1	1	1
35.	2	9	9	9	9	1	3	1	1	2	9	1	2	2	3	2	2	4	9	1	2	2	9	9	9
36.	5	1	2	1	1	1	1	1	1	3	2	9	2	2	3	6	2	4	1	1	9	1	2	1	1
37.	4	1	9	9	9	1	1	1	3	9	9	1	2	3	3	2	3	9	1	9	1	9	9	9	1
38.	2	2	9	2	1	1	3	1	1	2	9	9	9	9	2	3	3	3	2	2	9	9	9	9	1
39.	1	1	9	1	1	2	1	1	1	2	9	9	9	9	2	1	2	9	9	1	9	9	9	9	1
40.	3	9	1	2	1	1	1	1	1	4	9	9	9	1	2	5	2	9	1	2	2	2	1	1	2
41.	5	2	2	2	1	1	1	1	1	3	2	2	1	2	3	6	3	4	1	2	2	1	1	1	1
42.	2	2	2	9	9	1	2	3	1	2	1	9	2	9	4	3	3	9	2	1	9	9	2	9	9
43.	4	2	2	1	2	1	1	2	2	2	9	2	9	2	7	2	4	9	1	1	1	2	9	2
44.	3	1	1	9	9	1	3	1	1	3	1	9	1	1	2	3	3	3	2	1	1	2	1	2
45.	2	2	1	1	1	2	2	1	1	2	2	1	2	1	2	2	3	4	2	1	2	2	2	1	9
46.	4	2	2	2	1	1	1	1	4	9	9	9	4	6	2	9	9	1	2	1	1	9	2
47.	2	9	9	9	9	1	1	1	1	3	9	9	2	9	4	4	2	9	9	1	1	1	1	9	2
48.	1	9	9	9	9	2	2	1	1	2	1	1	2	9	2	2	2	9	9	1	2	1	2	2	9
49.	2	2	2	1	2	1	2	1	1	2	1	1	1	4	2	2	1	1	1	1	2	1	1
50.	4	2	2	2	1	1	3	1	1	3	2	2	9	3	3	2	9	2	1	2	2	2	9	1
51.	2	2	9	9	9	1	2	1	1	2	9	9	9	9	4	9	3	4	9	9	9	1	9	9	2
52.	1	2	1	9	9	1	1	1	1	2	1	1	2	1	2	3	3	1	1	2	2	2	1	9
53.	2	1	1	1	1	1	1	1	1	2	1	2	2	1	4	2	2	2	1	1	1	2	1	1
54.	4	2	9	9	9	1	2	1	1	2	2	9	9	9	3	3	2	4	1	1	9	9	9	9	1
55.	3	1	1	9	9	1	3	3	1	2	9	9	2	9	2	3	2	3	9	2	9	2	9	9	9
56.	3	1	1	9	9	1	2	2	1	2	9	9	9	9	3	3	3	3	9	1	2	9	9	1
57.	3	1	1	1	1	1	1	1	1	3	1	1	1	3	4	1	1	1	1	2	2	1	1	9
58.	1	2	9	9	9	2	2	2	1	1	2	9	2	2	3	2	2	1	1	1	2	2	1
59.	4	2	2	1	1	2	1	1	2	9	9	2	2	2	6	2	9	9	2	1	1	2	9	9
60.	4	1	2	1	2	1	1	1	1	2	2	9	2	2	3	7	2	4	1	1	1	1	2	1	1
61.	4	1	2	2	1	1	1	1	1	3	2	1	2	2	3	6	2	2	2	2	2	3	1	1
62.	4	9	9	9	9	1	1	1	1	2	1	1	9	9	4	7	3	3	9	9	9	9	9	9	1
63.	2	2	1	1	1	1	2	1	1	2	1	1	2	9	2	2	1	1	1	1	2	1	2	1	1
64.	3	1	1	9	9	1	1	1	1	1	1	9	9	9	2	3	1	1	1	1	1	9	1	9
65.	2	2	1	1	2	1	1	1	1	4	9	9	1	9	1	9	2	2	9	9	1	1	2	1	1
66.	4	9	9	2	1	1	1	1	1	3	2	1	9	2	3	6	2	4	9	1	1	1	3	1	9

```
29 30 31 32 33 34 35 36 37 38 39 40 41 42 43 44 45 46 47 48 49 50 51 52 53 54 55
 9  2  1  9  5  9  9  9  9  9  1  4  2  9  1  1  3  2  1  2  3  3  3  1  2  1  1
 1  2  2  2  2  9  2  2  9  2  1  2  5  1  1  1  3  2  2  3  3  3  2  1  4  1  2
 2  9  9  9  9  9  9  9  9  9  1  9  9  9  9  4  1  1  1  2  3  2  1  1  3  1
 9  2  2  1  4  2  9  9  9  9  3  3  4  1  1  1  3  2  2  3  3  3  3  1  1  3
 9  2  9  9  3  1  2  9  2  2  3  9  5  1  1  3  3  2  1  2  3  3  3  4  1  1  3
 9  9  9  9  4  9  9  9  9  9  4  9  9  9  9  1  1  1  1  1  2  4  3  1  1  1
 1  2  1  9  2  2  9  9  9  9  4  4  3  9  1  1  5  1  1  1  1  3  3  1  1  3
 1  1  1  9  4  2  9  9  9  9  1  9  9  9  1  1  5  2  1  1  1  2  3  1  1  1
 1  2  1  2  9  9  9  9  9  9  9  9  9  9  9  3  2  2  2  3  2  1  4  1  3
 1  1  2  2  1  2  2  9  2  1  9  5  3  1  1  3  1  1  1  1  3  2  3  1  1  2
 2  1  2  2  2  1  2  2  9  2  1  9  9  3  3  1  2  3  2  1  1  3  4  1  2  1  3
 9  9  9  9  9  9  9  9  9  9  1  9  9  9  1  1  5  2  2  3  3  4  2  3  1  1  3
 1  1  2  2  2  2  2  2  9  1  9  9  9  9  1  3  1  1  1  1  1  4  3  1  1  2
 2  1  1  2  5  9  9  9  9  9  3  3  5  1  3  1  1  1  1  1  1  4  1  2  1  3
 1  1  1  1  5  1  1  1  1  1  3  9  9  1  9  3  2  2  1  2  2  2  4  1  1  3
 1  2  2  9  4  9  9  9  9  9  1  4  3  1  1  1  2  3  1  1  2  1  4  1  4  1  1
 9  2  9  9  9  9  9  9  9  9  1  4  2  3  1  9  3  2  2  3  3  3  2  1  2  1  1
 9  9  9  9  9  9  9  9  9  9  1  9  9  9  9  9  3  2  1  1  1  1  2  4  1  1  1
 1  2  1  2  1  1  1  1  1  1  3  3  2  1  1  4  2  1  1  1  2  2  3  1  1  1
 2  2  2  2  2  9  2  2  2  9  1  9  9  9  1  1  3  1  1  1  1  3  2  3  1  1  3
 1  1  2  1  2  2  2  9  9  2  3  2  5  1  3  3  1  1  1  1  1  1  3  1  1  1
 1  1  1  9  9  9  9  9  9  9  1  2  5  1  1  1  3  2  2  3  4  3  2  3  1  1  3
 9  9  9  9  9  9  9  9  9  9  9  9  9  9  9  3  2  1  1  1  1  2  1  1  2  1
 9  9  9  2  3  1  2  9  9  2  9  1  2  5  1  3  1  4  2  1  1  3  1  3  1  2  3
 9  2  9  9  3  2  2  2  2  2  3  9  5  2  2  3  3  2  1  2  3  3  3  2  4  1  1  3
 9  2  9  2  5  1  1  1  1  1  1  2  5  1  3  1  4  2  1  1  1  3  3  1  1  2
 1  1  2  2  3  2  2  9  2  4  9  5  1  9  9  3  2  2  1  1  1  3  1  2  1  2
 2  9  9  9  5  9  9  9  9  9  4  9  9  1  1  1  3  2  1  1  2  1  3  3  1  1  3
 9  9  2  2  9  9  9  9  9  1  2  5  1  1  1  3  2  1  1  1  1  3  1  3  1  3
 1  1  1  9  2  9  2  9  2  9  1  9  9  9  9  9  1  1  1  1  3  1  2  1  2  1  1
 2  9  9  9  9  9  9  9  4  9  9  1  9  9  1  9  3  2  2  3  2  3  4  4  1  1  3
 9  2  9  9  2  9  9  9  9  9  1  9  4  1  3  1  4  2  1  1  3  3  2  1  1  2  1
 1  1  1  9  9  9  9  9  9  9  5  9  5  1  1  1  4  2  1  1  2  1  4  1  3
 1  1  1  3  1  2  2  9  2  1  2  5  1  3  3  4  2  1  1  1  3  3  1  1  2
 1  2  2  2  4  2  2  9  2  9  3  9  9  9  1  1  1  3  1  1  3  3  3  4  1  1  1
 1  1  1  9  4  1  2  2  2  9  3  9  9  3  1  1  1  1  1  1  4  1  2  1  3
 9  9  9  1  9  9  9  9  9  1  9  5  1  3  3  1  1  1  1  1  4  3  1  1  1
 9  9  9  1  2  1  2  2  9  9  4  2  5  1  2  1  1  2  1  1  3  1  4  1  4  1  3
 1  1  1  1  5  9  9  1  1  1  4  2  5  2  3  1  4  2  1  1  1  3  3  2  1  4  1  3
 1  1  1  3  1  2  2  9  2  1  2  5  1  3  3  4  2  1  1  1  3  3  1  1  2
 1  2  2  2  4  2  2  9  2  9  3  9  9  9  1  1  1  3  1  1  3  3  3  4  1  1  1
 1  1  1  9  4  1  2  2  2  9  3  9  9  3  1  1  1  1  1  1  4  1  2  1  3
 9  9  9  1  9  9  9  9  9  1  9  5  1  3  3  1  1  1  1  1  4  3  1  1  1
 9  2  5  9  2  9  9  2  9  9  4  2  5  1  3  1  3  1  2  2  1  3  3  3  1  1  3
```

References

Aberle, David F.
    1961   "Matrilineal descent in cross-cultural perspective," in David M. Schneider and Kathleen Gough, eds., *Matrilineal Kinship*, Berkeley, University of California Press: 655-727.

Ackerman, Charles
    1964   "Structure and statistics: the Purum case," *American Anthropologist 66:* 53-65.

Bachofen, Johann J.
    1861   *Das Mutterrecht*, Stuttgart, Krais & Hoffmann.

Barnett, Homer G.
    1949   *Palauan society*, Eugene, University of Oregon Publications.

Beaton, A. C.
    1943   "The Fur," *Sudan Notes and Records 29:* 1-39.

Bessac, Frank
    1968   "Cultunit and ethnic unit—processes and symbolism," in June Helm, ed., *Essays on the Problem of Tribe*, Proceedings of the 1967 Annual Spring Meeting of the American Ethnological Society, Seattle, University of Washington Press: 58-71.

Bettelheim, Bruno
    1962   *Symbolic wounds*, rev. ed., New York, Collier Books.

Blalock, Hubert M., Jr.
    1964   *Causal inferences in non-experimental research*, Chapel Hill, University of North Carolina Press.

Bock, Philip M.
    1967   "Love magic, menstrual taboos, and the facts of geography," *American Anthropologist 69:* 213-17.

Burling, Robbins
1963 *Rengsanggri: family and kinship in a Garo village*, Philadelphia, University of Pennsylvania Press.

Cohen, Ronald, and Alice Schlegel, with the assistance of Lawrence F. Felt and Earle Carlson
1968 "The tribe as a socio-political unit: a cross-cultural examination," in June Helm, ed., *Essays on the Problem of Tribe*, Proceedings of the 1967 Spring Meeting of the American Ethnological Society, Seattle, University of Washington Press: 120-49.

Cohen, Yehudi A.
1964 *The transition from childhood to adolescence; cross-cultural studies of initiation ceremonies, legal systems, and incest taboos*, Chicago, Aldine.

Condominas, Georges
1957 *Nous avons mangé la forêt*, Paris, Mercure de France.

Cooley, William W., and Paul R. Lohnes
1962 *Multivariate procedures for the behavioral sciences*, New York, John Wiley and Sons.

Coult, Allan D.
1962 "An analysis of Needham's critique of the Homans & Schneider theory," *Southwestern Journal of Anthropology 18:* 317-35.

Devereux, George
1950 "The psychology of feminine genital bleeding," *International Journal of Psycho-Analysis 31:* 237-57.

Douglas, Mary
1969 "Is matriliny doomed in Africa?" in Mary Douglas and Phyllis M. Kaberry, *Man in Africa*, London, Tavistock.

Eggan, Fred
1950 *Social organization of the Western Pueblos*, Chicago, University of Chicago Press.

Elkin, Adolphus P.
1938 "Kinship in South Australia," *Oceania 9:* 41-78.

Ember, Melvin
1963 "The relationship between economic and political development in non-industrialized societies," *Ethnology 2:* 228-48.

1969 "The conditions favoring first-cousin marriage," paper read at the Annual Meetings of the American Anthropological Association, New Orleans.

Eyde, David B., and Paul M. Postal
    1961   "Avunculocality and incest: the development of unilateral cross-cousin marriage and Crow-Omaha kinship systems," *American Anthropologist 63:* 747-71.

Felkin, Robert W.
    1885   "Notes on the For tribe of Central Africa," *Royal Society of Edinburgh, Proceedings, 13:* 205-65.

Force, Roland W.
    1960   "Leadership and culture change in Palau," *Fieldiana: Anthropology 50.*

Ford, Clellan S.
    1945   "A comparative study of human reproduction," *Yale University Publications in Anthropology 32.*

Fox, Robin
    1967   *Kinship and marriage: an anthropological perspective,* Baltimore, Penguin Books.

Frazer, James G.
    1907-27   *The golden bough,* 3d ed., 12 vols., London, Macmillan (1st ed. 1890).

Fromm, Erich
    1941   *Escape from freedom,* New York, Farrar and Rinehart.

Gardiner, J. Stanley
    1898   "The natives of Rotuma," *Anthropological Institute of Great Britain and Ireland, Journal 27:* 396-435, 457-524.

Garfield, Viola, et al.
    1951   "The Tsimshian, their arts and music," *American Ethnological Society, Publication 18.*

Gough, Kathleen
    1961a   "Nayar: Central Kerala," in David M. Schneider and Kathleen Gough, eds., *Matrilineal Kinship,* Berkeley, University of California Press: 298-384.
    1961b   "The modern disintegration of matrilineal descent groups," in David M. Schneider and Kathleen Gough, eds., *Matrilineal Kinship,* Berkeley, University of California Press: 631-52.

Grinnell, George B.
    1891   "Marriage among the Pawnees," *American Anthropologist 4:* 275-81.

Hall, K. R. L., and Irven Devore
1965   "Baboon social behavior," in Irven Devore, ed., *Primate Behavior*, New York, Holt, Rinehart and Winston: 53-110.

Harris, Marvin
1968   *The rise of anthropological theory*, New York, Thomas Y. Crowell.

Hobhouse, Leonard T.
1924   *Morals in evolution: a study in comparative ethics*, 4th ed., New York, Henry Holt.

Holmberg, Allan R.
1950   "Nomads of the long bow; the Siriono of Eastern Bolivia," *Smithsonian Institution, Institute of Social Anthropology, Publication 10.*

Homans, George C., and David M. Schneider
1955   *Marriage, authority, and final causes: a study of unilateral cross-cousin marriage*, Glencoe, Free Press.

Honigmann, John J.
1949   "Culture and ethos of Kaska society," *Yale University Publications in Anthropology 40.*
1954   "The Kaska Indians: an ethnographic reconstruction," *Yale University Publications in Anthropology 51.*

Howitt, Alfred W.
1890   "The Dieri and other kindred tribes of Central Australia," *Anthropological Institute of Great Britain and Ireland, Journal 20:* 30-104.

Hsu, Francis L. K.
1965   "The effect of dominant kinship relationships on kin and non-kin behavior: a hypothesis," *American Anthropologist 67:* 638-61.

Jay, Phyllis
1965   "The common langur of North India," in Irven Devore, ed., *Primate Behavior*, New York, Holt, Rinehart and Winston: 197-249.

Köbben, André J.
1952   "New ways of presenting an old idea: the statistical method in social anthropology," *Royal Anthropological Institute of Great Britain and Ireland, Journal 82:* 129-46 (reprinted in Moore 1966, pp. 166-92).

Koyama, Takashi
> 1962   "Changing family structure in Japan," in Robert J. Smith and Richard K. Beardsley, eds., *Japanese Culture: Its Development and Characteristics*, Chicago, Aldine: 47-54.

Labouret, Henri
> 1931   "Les tribus du rameau lobi," *Paris, Université, Institut d'Ethnologie, Travaux et Mémoires 15.*

Lane, Robert B.
> 1962   "Patrilateral cross-cousin marriage: structural analysis and ethnographic cases," *Ethnology 1:* 467-99.

Leach, Edmund R.
> 1951   "The structural implications of matrilateral cross-cousin marriage," *Royal Anthropological Institute of Great Britain and Ireland, Journal 81:* 23-55.
> 1961   "Rethinking anthropology," in his *Rethinking Anthropology*, London, Athlone Press: 1-27 (paperback edition 1966).

Lévi-Strauss, Claude
> 1949   *Les structures élémentaires de la parenté*, Paris, Presses Universitaires de France.
> 1963   "Structural analysis in linguistics and anthropology," in his *Structural Anthropology*, New York, Basic Books: 31-54.
> 1969   *The elementary structures of kinship*, London, Eyre and Spottiswoode (see especially "Preface to the second edition").

Lewis, Oscar
> 1951   *Life in a Mexican village: Tepoztlan restudied*, Urbana, University of Illinois Press.

Loeb, Edwin M.
> 1962   "In feudal Africa," *International Journal of American Linguistics 28, no. 3, pt. 2.*

Lowie, Robert H.
> 1918   "Myths and traditions of the Crow Indians," *American Museum of Natural History, Anthropological Papers, 25:* 1-308.

Malinowski, Bronislaw
> 1931   "Culture," in Edwin R. A. Seligman and Alvin Johnson, eds., *Encyclopedia of the Social Sciences 4*, New York, Macmillan: 621-46.
> 1953   *Sex and repression in savage society*, London, Routledge and Kegan Paul (originally published in 1927).

Mitchell, James Clyde
1956 *The Yao village: a study in the social structure of a Nyasa-land tribe*, Manchester, published on behalf of the Rhodes-Livingstone Institute by Manchester University Press.

Moerman, Michael
1965 "Ethnic identification in a complex civilization: Who are the Lue?" *American Anthropologist 67:* 1215-30.
1968 "Being Lue: uses and abuses of ethnic identification," in June Helm, ed., *Essays on the Problem of Tribe*, Proceedings of the 1967 Annual Spring Meeting of the American Ethnological Society, Seattle, University of Washington Press: 153-69.

Moore, Frank W., ed.
1966 *Readings in cross-cultural methodology* (2d printing, reset), New Haven, HRAF Press.

Morgan, Lewis H.
1881 "Houses and house life of the American aborigines," *U.S. Geographical and Geological Survey of the Rocky Mountain Region, Contributions to North American Ethnology 4.*

Mountford, Charles P.
1958 *The Tiwi; their art, myth, and ceremony*, London, Phoenix House.

Murdock, George Peter
1940 "The Cross-Cultural Survey," *American Sociological Review 5:* 361-70.
1949 *Social structure*, New York, Macmillan.
1957 "World ethnographic sample," *American Anthropologist 59:* 664-87.
1966a "The Cross-Cultural Survey," in Frank W. Moore, ed., *Readings in Cross-Cultural Methodology* (reset edition), New Haven, HRAF Press: 40-49.
1966b "World ethnographic sample," in Frank W. Moore, ed., *Readings in Cross-Cultural Methodology* (reset edition), New Haven, HRAF Press: 195-220.
1967 *Ethnographic atlas: a summary*, Pittsburgh, University of Pittsburgh Press.
1968 "World sampling provinces," *Ethnology 7:* 305-26.

Murdock, George Peter, et al.
1962- "Ethnographic atlas," *Ethnology 1* to date.

Nakane, Chie
   1967   *Garo and Khasi: a comparative study in matrilineal systems*, Paris and The Hague, Mouton.

Naroll, Raoul
   1962   *Data quality control—a new research technique: prolegomena to a cross-cultural study of culture stress*, New York, Free Press of Glencoe.
   1964   "On ethnic unit classification," *Current Anthropology 5:* 283-312.
   1965   "Galton's problem: the logic of cross-cultural analysis," *Social Research 32:* 428-51.
   1967   "Native concepts and cross-cultural surveys," *American Anthropologist 69:* 511-12.
   1968   "Who the Lue are," in June Helm, ed., *Essays in the Problem of Tribe*, Proceedings of the 1967 Annual Spring Meeting of the American Ethnological Society, Seattle, University of Washington Press: 72-79.
   1970   "What have we learned from cross-cultural surveys?" *American Anthropologist 72:* 1227-88.

Naroll, Raoul, Winston Alnot, Janice Caplan, Judith F. Hansen, Jeanne Maxant, and Nancy Schmidt
   1970   "A standard ethnographic sample: preliminary edition," *Current Anthropology 11:* 235-48.

Needham, Rodney
   1962   *Structure and sentiment*, Chicago, University of Chicago Press.

Oliver, Douglas
   1955   *A Solomon Island society*, Cambridge, Harvard University Press.

Radcliffe-Brown, Alfred R.
   1952   "The mother's brother in South Africa," in his *Structure and Function in Primitive Society*, Glencoe, Free Press: 15-31 (originally issued in 1924).

Redfield, Robert
   1930   *Tepoztlan, a Mexican village: a study of folk life*, Chicago, University of Chicago Press.

Richards, Audrey I.
   1950   "Some types of family structure amongst the Central Bantu," in Alfred R. Radcliffe-Brown and C. Daryll Forde, eds., *African Systems of Kinship and Marriage*, London, Oxford University Press for the International African Institute: 207-51.

Ronhaar, Jan Hermann
1931   *Woman in primitive motherright societies*, The Hague, J. B. Wolters.

Sade, Donald S.
1968   "Inhibition of son-mother mating among free-ranging rhesus monkeys," *Science and Psychoanalysis 12:* 18-37.

Schaller, George B.
1965   "The behavior of the mountain gorilla," in Irven Devore, ed., *Primate Behavior*, New York, Holt, Rinehart and Winston: 324-67.

Schneider, David M., and Kathleen Gough, eds.
1961   *Matrilineal kinship*, Berkeley, University of California Press.

Slater, Mariam K.
1959   "Ecological factors in the origin of incest," *American Anthropologist 61:* 1042-59.

Speck, Frank G.
1907   "The Creek Indians of Taskigi Town," *American Anthropological Association, Memoir 2:* 99-164.

Stephens, William N.
1961   "A cross-cultural study of menstrual taboos," *Genetic Psychology Monographs 64:* 385-416 (reprinted in Clellan S. Ford, ed., *Cross-Cultural Approaches*, New Haven, HRAF Press, 1967: 67-94).

1962   *The Oedipus complex: cross-cultural evidence*, New York, Free Press of Glencoe.

1963   *The family in cross-cultural perspective*, New York, Holt, Rinehart and Winston.

Stephens, William N., and Roy G. D'Andrade
1962   "Kin-avoidance," in William N. Stephens, *The Oedipus Complex: Cross-Cultural Evidence*, New York, Free Press of Glencoe: 124-50.

Stevenson, Robert F.
1968   *Population and political systems in tropical Africa*, New York, Columbia University Press.

Stone, Doris Z.
1962   "The Talamancan tribes of Costa Rica," *Harvard University, Peabody Museum of American Archaeology and Ethnology, Papers 43, no. 2.*

Suguru, Kenichi, and Harumi Befu
1962   "Kinship organization of the Sara Ainu," *Ethnology 1:* 287-98.

Swanton, John R.
1924-25 "Social organization and social usages of the Indians of the Creek Confederacy," *U.S. Bureau of American Ethnology, Annual Report 42:* 23-472, 859-900.

Thurston, Edgar
1909 *Castes and tribes of Southern India*, Madras, Government Press.

Tylor, Edward B.
1889 "On a method of investigating the development of institutions: applied to laws of marriage and descent," *Anthropological Institute of Great Britain and Ireland, Journal 18:* 245-72 (reprinted in Moore 1966: 1-25).

Weltfish, Gene
1965 *The lost universe*, New York, Basic Books.

Westermarck, Edward
1921 *The history of human marriage*, 5th ed., 3 vols., London, Macmillan (1st ed. published in 1891).

White, Leslie A.
1948 "The definition and prohibition of incest," *American Anthropologist, n.s. 50:* 416-35.

Whiting, John W. M., and Irvin L. Child
1953 *Child training and personality: a cross-cultural study*, New Haven, Yale University Press.

Wolf, Arthur P.
1966 "Childhood association, sexual attraction, and the incest taboo: a Chinese case," *American Anthropologist 68:* 883-98.
1970 "Childhood association and sexual attraction: a further test of the Westermarck hypothesis," *American Anthropologist 72:* 503-15.

Young, Frank, and Albert A. Bacdayan
1965 "Menstrual taboos and social rigidity," *Ethnology 4:* 225-40 (reprinted in Clellan S. Ford, ed., *Cross-Cultural Approaches*, New Haven, HRAF Press, 1967: 95-110).

Index

Descent groups, cohesiveness of, 82, 83
Descent systems, 138-39, 140-44; conflicts of, 140; matrilineal, 142-44; reality of, 140, 142
Dieri, 38, 51
Diffusion, independent, 55-57
Disagreement, coder, 52-53; source, 50-52
Divorce, 62-63, 101-06. *See also* Marriage
Dominance, Brother, 59-86, 88, 91-92, 94-95, 97-99, 100-06, 112-18, 121, 123-33, 134-36, 138, 143 passim; Husband, 59-86, 88, 94, 95-99, 100-06, 112-14, 121, 122-33, 134-36, 138, 143 passim; Male, 80ff., 97-98 passim; Neither, 59-86, 94-95, 98-99, 100-06, 123, 131, 134-35, 143 passim
Dominant dyads, 15n., 113
Duolocal residence, 4, 78, 83
Dyads, dominant, 15n., 113

Error, 46-57; coder's, 38, 43; in coding, 50-53, 56-57; ethnographer's, 38; in interpretation, 53-57; random, 46; at source, 46-50, 56-57; systematic, 46
Ethnographer, errors of, 38; sex of, 47, 49-50

Factor analyses, 99-106
Female autonomy, 22-26, 87-90 passim
Fisher's Exact Test, 45, 55-56, 60, 68, 69

Ga, 83n.
Galton's problem, 28, 29, 31, 33, 35
Garo, 4, 39, 51, 61, 112, 114-16
Goajiro, 32, 34
Groom capture, 39, 61
Guanche, 35
Gure, 42

Herero, 141
Hopi, 3, 7-8, 9, 12-13, 19, 20, 22, 32-33, 38, 42, 89-90, 125, 143-44

Human Relations Area Files, 28, 37
Husband Dominant. *See* Dominance

Incest, 96-97; father-daughter, 96-97; sibling, 26, 76, 90-91
Incest taboo, 12-13, 69-70, 76, 91, 122-33, 135-36; Augustinian theory, 125; demographic theory, 128n.; family disruption theory, 126-27; hypotheses about direction of, 129; revulsion theory, 126; social distance theory, 127
Independent diffusion, 55-57
Integration, political. *See* Political integration
Interpretation, error in, 53-57
Iroquois, 51

Japanese, 83n., 134
Jealousy. *See* Co-wife jealousy

Kaska, 90, 112
Khasi, 4, 7, 20, 22, 38
Kunama, 34
Kurtatchi, 53

Lakalai, 38
Lesu, 53
Lineages, ranked, 82, 116-20
Linked Pair test, 55-56
Lobi, 38, 111, 118-20
Locono, 35, 38
Longudu, 34, 49
Luguru, 34

Mandan, 32
Marriage, cross-cousin, 10-11, 68, 71, 84, 86, 90, 96, 101-06, 107-21, 135-36; disruption of, 63, 73, 101-06, 112; preferential, 26; plural, 23, 87-88; uncle-niece, 110
Matriarchy, 1
Matrilineal descent, studies of, 1-5
Matrilineal puzzle, 1, 3, 5, 11, 85, 97, 121, 134, 137, 140-41
Matrilocal residence, 4, 71-72, 82-84, 98-99, 101-06